# The New Jersey House

# The New Jersey House

Helen Schwartz
Photographs by
Margaret Morgan Fisher

Rutgers University Press
New Brunswick, New Jersey

Manufactured in the United States of America

*Library of Congress Cataloging in Publication Data*

Schwartz, Helen, 1935–
The New Jersey house.

Bibliography:p.
1. Dwellings—New Jersey—Guide-books.
2. New Jersey—Description and travel—1951–
Guide-books. I. Fisher, Margaret Morgan.
II. Title
NA7235.N5S36 1983 728′.09749 82-7552
ISBN 0-8135-0965-3 AACR2
ISBN 0-8135-0990-4 (pbk.)

A good house is a powerful means of civilization . . . when smiling lawns and tasteful cottages begin to embellish a country we know that order and culture are established. . . . It is the solitude and freedom of the family home in the country which constantly preserve the purity of the nation and invigorate its intellectual powers.

Andrew Jackson Downing,
*The Architecture of Country Houses* (1850)

# Contents

# Preface

Although New Jersey is the nation's most urban state, with much of its material past buried under highways, shopping centers, and major subdivisions, a surprising number of houses that were built during the first century of colonization are still standing. An even larger number of dwellings built during America's first 150 years can be found throughout the state. In some of the smaller cities and larger towns, entire neighborhoods appear much as they did before World War I.

Until recently, this great wealth of architecture remained largely unremarked, despite the fact that it reflects the formation and development of both state and nation. Although this book was first envisioned as a simple description of the state's domestic architecture, it soon became apparent that there could be no such thing as simplicity when architecture was the subject.

In doing my research I discovered that available information was spotty, at best. Instead of an orderly progression of documented facts I found a patchwork of information composed of scholarship, supposition, and some bits that could only be described as conjecture. There were and remain gaps in the architectural portrait of this state. The complex beginnings, later rapid urbanization, and indifference to New Jersey's architecture that existed for many years combined to blur and sometimes erase any picture we might have of our architectural past.

All of this considered, it is still possible to learn a good deal and see quite a few houses that reflect earlier life. During the year that I spent traveling throughout New Jersey I discovered rich concentrations of interesting houses all over the state—often unknown to the general public. It was often easier to locate these houses than to pin down the date of construction or the origins of the building traditions. Frequently my research led me to dead ends and gaps in architectural records. Among a diverse body of data I found excellent pieces of scholarship but also a fair amount of myth and rumor. Separating the two was difficult. There were houses with ambitious dates set by overly optimistic owners eager to live in an "old house." These were more than compensated for by houses that had been carefully documented and researched. I puzzled my way through agreements and disagreements between scholars and, in the process, learned that no matter how many facts there were, an almost equal number of qualifiers remained and there was usually at least one authority who would disagree with any statement.

Unanswered questions and ambiguous information notwithstanding, the houses of New Jersey speak for themselves. Along with an insufficiency of fact there exists an abundance of architectural riches. Even though this book was not intended to serve as a guidebook, there are, in fact, so many architecturally significant concentrations of houses that I believed that many of the towns merited more than a simple listing. As a result, the book was expanded to include capsule descriptions of many architecturally rich communities and serve as an architectural gazetteer, so that these descriptions could become architectural reality to anyone who cared to find them.

Many people have been helpful. I have been moved by the generosity and goodwill with which they gave their time and knowledge. They have been generous in their willingness to help with the small problems as well as in discovering the larger ideas.

In order to learn about the great, often undocumented treasure that is New Jersey's architecture, I began by surveying almost two hundred of the state's historical societies. Members were generous with their time, taking me to houses and out-of-the-way places that might otherwise have remained unknown to me. They also shared their appreciation and enthusiasm—a sharing which has, for me, been as valuable as the acquisition of knowledge.

In preparing this book I also consulted with historians, public officials, architects, and preservationists. Early journals, books, magazines, pattern books from the eighteenth and nineteenth centuries, old maps and atlases, together with newspapers and the data in the state and national registers of historic houses and the Historic American Building Survey of the Library of Congress combined to create a picture of New Jersey domestic architecture. I appreciate the help I received from county cultural and heritage commissions and the many libraries and their staffs and various colleges and organizations throughout the state who share my concern that the domestic architecture of New Jersey be properly understood and appreciated. I am especially grateful to Margaret Bolton; Roxanne Carkhuff, Hunterdon County Cultural and Heritage Commission; Robert Judson Clark, Princeton University; David Cohen, New Jersey Historical Commission; Arlene Dempsey, Boonton Historical Society; Barbara Ervin, New Jersey Historical Society; Joseph Felcone of Princeton; John Grady, Plainfield Heritage Associates; Constance Grieff, Heritage Associates; Betty Hahle, Riverton Historical Society; John Hammond, Monmouth Historical Society; Clark Hutchinson; J. Louise Jost, Shrewsbury Historical Society; Terry Karchner, New Jersey Department of Environmental Protection; Dr. Nicholas Mamaras, Burlington City Historical Society; Malcolm Knowles of Crosswicks; George Moss, Jr., of Rumson; Ferris Olin, Rutgers University; Thomas Peterson, Hillsboro Planning Administration; Judith Pinch, Woodrow Wilson National Fellowship Foundation; Eleanor Price, New Jersey Society of Architectural Historians; Steve Richer, New Jersey Department of Tourism; Jean Ricker, Boonton Historical Society; Donald Sinclair, New Jersey Collection, Rutgers University Library; Jack Steinberg, Ocean Grove Historical Society; Claire Tholl, Bergen County Office of Cultural and Heritage Affairs; Stephanie Toothman, National Register of Historic Places; and special thanks to Helen Hamilton and Karen Perry, without whose help and support this book would have been far less than it is.

# The New Jersey House

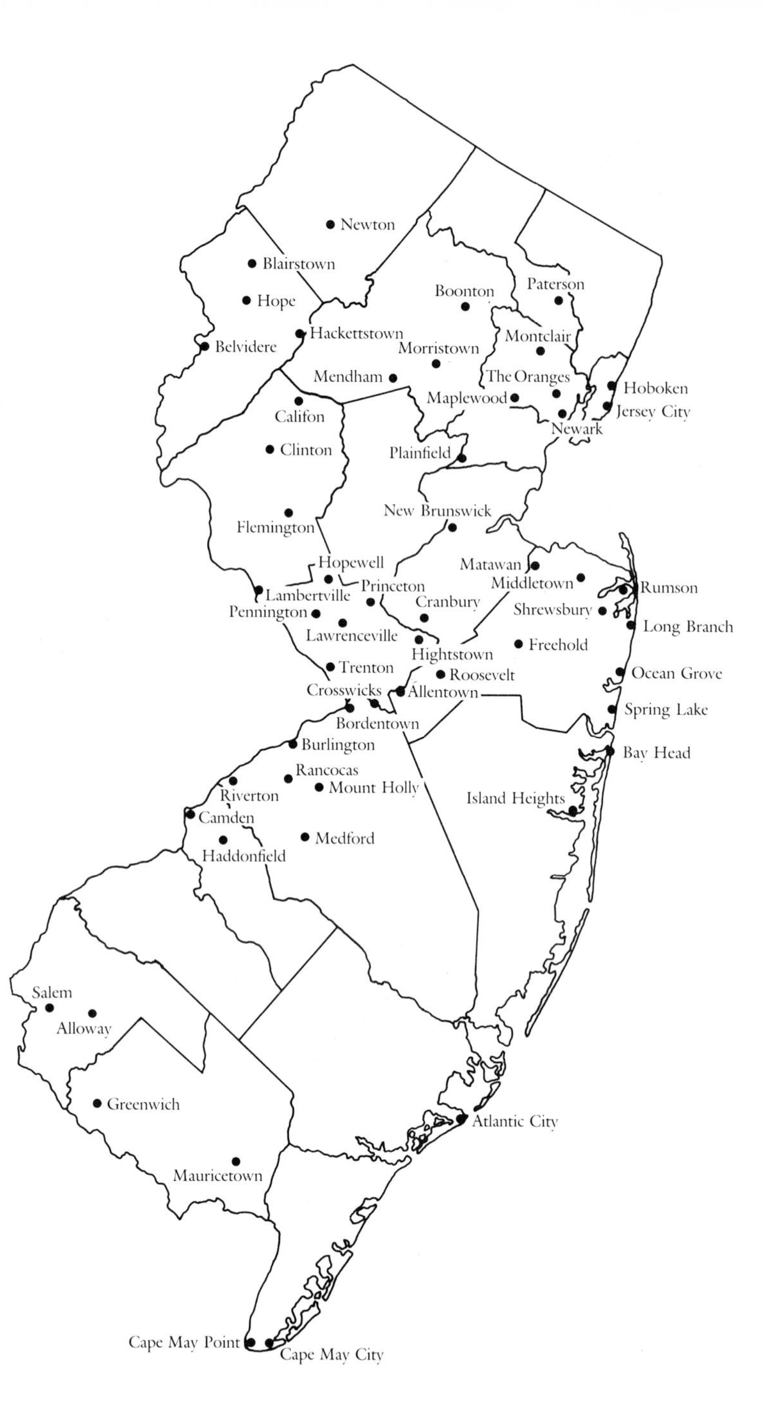


*Towns of special interest in New Jersey*

# Settlement Patterns

The early New Jersey houses that have survived reflect the settlement patterns of the many different Europeans who first settled in the state. Dutch doors, Flemish-bond brickwork, German cut stone, English ornamental brickwork, and Swedish plank construction are among the European-inspired elements they brought with them.

*Hancock's Bridge.* In the seventeenth century, early Swedish settlers built their houses using cedar logs cut from trees that had been preserved in the swamps for centuries. The wood was often made into planks to build houses that were similar to this reconstruction of a one-room cabin.

2

*Mount Holly.* Log construction was another traditional building mode used by the Swedes during their early years in the colony.

*Mannington.* Very little evidence of early log and plank houses survives. The few such remaining houses have frequently been incorporated into later, larger structures that often mask the lines of the original building. Here, the frame wing encloses a cabin built many years earlier in the Swedish mode. Although the exterior is changed, most of the interior elements have been preserved.

*Montville.* The earliest houses of the Dutch settlers were the simplest of structures. By the eighteenth century distinctive features such as the flaring bell eave became common Dutch Colonial characteristics.

*Boonton.* In the beginning the Dutch houses, like those of other settlement groups, were usually quite small. Larger additions were frequently added laterally to the original dwelling, extending the façade. The two sections of this house each have distinctive roof styles—flared eaves for the older part and a simple gambrel for the addition.

*Boonton.* Gable end windows were originally the sole source of attic light. The dormers found on most early Dutch houses are later additions. Some, such as this clearly Victorian dormer (right), contribute the stylistic imprint of another era.

8

*Rockleigh.* In Bergen County many fine examples of Dutch homes still stand. Most are in the river valleys, close to the roads, in what are now crowded suburban areas. Gambrel roofs, flaring eaves with deep overhangs, and an occasional front stoop make these houses easy to identify.

*Details.* There were few windows in the early houses. The divided door admitted additional light and air to the interiors. A flat arch made of brick was often used as a window head.

Despite their common language and many shared traditions, the English settlers were culturally diverse. Their complex cultural baggage included several architectural traditions: some had their origins on the Continent, some in Great Britain, others had been acquired in New England and on Long Island. Available materials and the traditions of neighboring settlement groups also influenced the appearance of the early English houses in New Jersey. Because of their complex heritage these houses are frequently difficult to identify or categorize.

*Burlington.* The variation in the brickwork work of the gable end of this late-seventeenth-century house reveals the ghost of the original roof line.

*Moorestown.* In many early houses there was no formal plan for the façade. Instead, windows were often randomly placed, reflecting the interior arrangement of rooms.

*Princeton.* Although most eighteenth-century houses have been altered over the years, many have preserved their distinctive simple lines. The stone house, which was once a blacksmith's residence, bears similarities to Quaker structures built outside New Jersey.

*Clinton.* Unlike New England houses, which were often enlarged by rear additions, early English-built New Jersey houses usually grew by lateral extensions of the original structure, as did houses built by other early settlers in the colony.

*Sergeantsville.* Houses in Hunterdon County, which once covered a goodly portion of New Jersey, were often built of abundant local stone by the Germans and the English.

*Middletown.* Monmouth County was settled early by the Dutch and English, whose building traditions often were blended in the early houses.

*Matawan.* Scalloped shingles found on pre-revolutionary dwellings were an American phenomenon referred to in early travel journals. This highly decorative form of construction was used on Monmouth County structures. Several remain, including the historic Allen house, Clinton house, and Burrowes mansion.

*Sergeantsville.* A number of methods were used to make early houses weather-tight. One frequently used device was the application of stucco over stone.

18

*North Crosswicks.* In early houses the first floor was often built close to the ground. Low ceilings were also common, and the two features combined to create the strong horizontal movements that disappeared only a few years later.

*Ringoes.* The appearance of the roof often provides clues to stylistic origins. Although the gambrel is associated with Dutch-built houses, the Swedish and English also used this roof style. Often the nature of the angle indicated the origin.

*Salem/Perth Amboy.* The long, sloping roof of the saltbox, or catslide, had its origins in New England. The silhouette was originally the result of a lean-to addition placed at the rear. It was so well liked that it was soon included as part of the original construction in many houses.

*Burlington*. The oldest section of this house was built in 1705. Like many of the "Southern bricks" the front door and lower windows are shielded by a pent roof.

In Southern New Jersey Quaker settlers built houses that were more stylistically homogeneous than those built elsewhere. They were often, but not always, symmetrical three-bay structures. Although there was an occasional frame or stone dwelling, brick was the most frequently used material.

*Details.* Brick was often laid in Flemish bond, with headers and stretchers alternating in the same course. Frequently the pattern was made using traditional bricks whose color was altered by overfiring to create a blue glaze.

Before the Revolution the crown levied a tax upon window glass. In some houses the windows were made smaller, while in others they were sealed over completely to reduce the size of the tax that the owner was required to pay.

On some of the Quaker houses, the brickwork on the gable ends was laid in an ornamental pattern.

*Salem County.* Many of the patterned-brick houses were modest Georgians with a central doorway. Sometimes there was also a smaller wing. The pattern used on the gable ends varied from house to house and was rarely repeated.

24

*Alloway*. The most elaborate of the ornamental bricks is the Dickinson house, which also claims the tallest date marking, extending a full seventeen courses. Its design is thought to include all the known brickwork patterns.

*Hope.* In the course of their wanderings Moravians established the village of Hope and lived there for a short time. They built an entire community using native stone for dwellings and community facilities constructed in the German vernacular mode.

*Boonton*. Some of the early German houses have one end built into a slope. They were generally built facing north and were called German bank houses. Those that remain were usually enlarged by the addition of wings that had the appearance of a complete house.

*Lawrence Township.* The three sections of this house (not all of which are shown in this photo) span a century. The taller, more elegant lines of the late Georgian section dwarf the central wing, which was built well before the Revolution.

*Titusville.* The date of construction is often indicated by a building's height. After the middle of the eighteenth century the first floor was usually built over a basement. A small flight of stairs at the entryway accommodated the higher floor level.

It is not easy to imagine the land between the Delaware and the Hudson as it was before the Europeans arrived. The houses, factories, and highways that cover much of twentieth-century New Jersey mask the open countryside, abundant forest, and uninterrupted shoreline that confronted early settlers over three hundred years ago.

What is now the most urban of the states was a wilderness. It was home to the Lenni Lenape, who carved out their lives from an untamed environment using only the simplest of tools. When the Europeans arrived in the seventeenth century, their mode of living was initially similar to that of the Indians. They made their homes in caves and earthen dugouts with roofs of sod and reeds or else constructed crude structures of tree bark. When they could, they built log huts with dirt floors. These were the first European-built houses in New Jersey.

The early houses, and those built for the succeeding hundred years, well into the eighteenth century, often incorporated structural elements resembling those the settlers had left behind. In this, the most culturally diverse of the colonies, building traditions of the Dutch, English, Swedes, Scots, and Germans, as well as colonial modes from New England, were adapted to local conditions. Architectural customs that had been part of the Old World often determined the appearance of roof lines, doorways, and floor plans, and the character of exterior surfaces. Many of the customs persisted for years and, in some cases, survive today.

The earliest New Jersey settlements were located along the colony's complex network of shoreline and harbors. It was not long, however, before the adventurous followed the rivers and traced Indian trails inland to establish new communities. Within a few years the narrow trails were widened and roads cut from the wilderness to link villages. By the time of the Revolution, New Jersey was home to an estimated hundred thousand people. Small cities, villages, and towns were well established throughout the state.

Many of these towns had formed around the colony's growing industries. Newark was an early leather-making center. There was a forge at Tinton Falls in 1674. Within fifty years of settlement, iron from local mines was also being processed in several locations to the north. In 1739, Caspar Wistar started the first successful glassworks in the colonies in Alloway. Farther south, Cape May became a whaling port.

As mining and industrial activity increased and commercial exchange grew between the colonies and England, the network of roads expanded. Trade routes crisscrossed the colony, and these in turn encouraged an even greater flow of people and goods. New Jersey soon assumed its long-standing role as a corridor state.

The same features that caused the colony to become a corridor also made its seaports and highways major routes for transmitting ideas into the interior. Elements of taste, culture, and news from across the ocean and from the other colonies almost always passed through New Jersey en route to the rest of the country. This traffic, in turn, generated even more roads, beginning a cycle of growth that continues today. More roads drew traffic and more people, encouraging the construction of houses and inns. Many of these houses built before and just after the Revolution still border the streets and highways that have replaced the early roads. They often stand close to the edge of busy roads, gentle reminders of earlier days.

## The First Houses

The first houses, built for temporary shelter, were primitive structures. Often, only a single room accommodated families while they cleared their land and established their herds. These houses were usually made of wood. Although none remain, we know something about them from the contents of old diaries, county histories, maps, letters, and travel accounts. The closest we come to seeing one—a Swedish cedar plank house—is the reconstructed cabin at Hancock's Bridge.

Isolated examples of houses built before 1700 do exist in New Jersey, but they are rare. In addition to reconstructions made on the basis of old documents, there are early houses that have been altered or incorporated into larger, newer structures and no longer appear as they once did. Although the very early houses appear simple, they are expressions of traditional forms. Essentially medieval, they were built using techniques that had been unchanged for hundreds of years. It is sometimes claimed that even their unrefined appearance was a deliberate expression of the medieval belief that the natural character of materials was a form of divine expression. Practical considerations, however, were probably as important as lofty ideals in determining the rough nature of these dwellings.

By the early eighteenth century New Jersey houses were sturdy enough to endure. Those that have survived reflect the complicated settlement patterns that shaped New Jersey. Dutch doors, Flemish-bond brickwork, German cut stone, English ornamented brickwork, and Swedish plank construction are among the European-inspired elements that connect these houses with the many different people who were the state's earliest citizens.

Most early New Jersey houses are grouped according to the European origins of the people who built them. There are usually specific architectural details connected with each group. The traditions that grew out of national origins, however, were not the only factors that shaped these houses. Available materials were sometimes more important than a builder's past. There were also occasions when traditions were shared, and the resulting blends created a new genre. For example, a house might be built for an English family by a Dutch mason, thus combining the traditions of both cultures. Because of these varied influences, a great many early houses do not fit easily into formal categories and are, instead, architectural hybrids.

After the first decades, concessions to architectural fashion became common place. Structural patterns were adapted, albeit modestly, to include elements of newer forms. Existing houses, too, were altered to conform to the passing style or updated when damaged or deteriorating sections were repaired. When wings were added to meet changing needs and reflect increased prosperity, this also became an occasion to add another, more up-to-date style to an existing dwelling. It is not unusual to find a pre-Revolution farmhouse that was spruced up a century later with the unlikely addition of a mansard roof or a gingerbread porch. During the Georgian era it was common practice to modernize houses by replacing original windows with more modern sashes composed of many small panes. A prospering business or a growing family were often the inspirations for additions that changed silhouettes and converted simple one-room structures to complex, multi-roomed houses. Occasionally an old house all but disappeared within the more stylish and grandiose additions that grew around it. Cedar log houses can be found within charming brick Federals. Georgian brick mansions often retain a tiny frame wing that was the original dwelling.

*The Scandinavian Heritage*. The "Swedes" were among the earliest groups to settle in New Jersey. Like many other settlement groups, they were, in fact, made up of people from more than one country. Included among them were a great many Finns, who contributed their own log traditions to the houses that are usually referred to today as Swedish. When the Swedes arrived they used ancient cedar logs, preserved for centuries in the swampy land, to build uncomplicated houses similar to those they had left behind. They notched the logs at the ends and filled the spaces with mortar. The travel journal of Jasper Danckerts describes a house near "Borlinghton" as "made according to the Swedish mode, and as they usually build their houses here, which are block houses, being nothing else than entire trees, split through the middle, or squared out of the rough, and placed in the form of a square, one upon the other, as high as they wish to have the house; the ends of these timbers are let into each other, about a foot from the ends, half of one into half of the other. The whole structure is thus made without a nail or a spike. The ceiling and the roof do not exhibit much finer work, except among the most careful people, who have the ceiling planked and a glass window. The doors are wide enough, but very low, so that you have to stoop in entering. These houses are quite tight and warm."

Swedish settlement was short-lived. Many of the original settlers departed, and those who did remain in the New World became acculturated to the dominant English mode. As a result, the plank house as well as most other expressions of Swedish culture all but disappeared.

*The Dutch Imprint*. The Dutch architectural influence upon New Jersey was much stronger. Hundreds of the houses that the early Dutch settlers built still stand in the northern and central parts of the state. In fact, Dutch impact even extended into the early twentieth century, when the "Dutch Colonial" style became as popular an American architectural form as the Georgian, and, later, the split-level and raised ranch houses.

Although the people called Dutch developed a style of house that was uniquely their own, the origins of their building traditions are not as easy to trace as those of the Swedes, and a European prototype for the "Dutch Colonial" is yet to be found. Because the "Dutch" were actually a combination of Walloons, Scandinavians, Germans, Huguenots, and Poles who had been assimilated into Dutch society in the New World, an elaborate mix of custom and experience combined to determine the appearance of their houses. Although considered by some to be the first indigenous American architectural form, Dutch houses were shaped by a blend of traditions that continues to puzzle folk historians.

There were few trees in the low countries. As a result, the Dutch had developed a masonry tradition that they continued in their new land when they could. In New Amsterdam and southern New York they built houses that resembled those they had left behind: steep roofs and stepped gables topped tall, narrow buildings with gable ends facing the street.

As the Dutch moved across the river from New York into New Jersey their house style changed from the steep-roofed, medieval urban form into a rural style—the familiar long, low cottage. Although the early settlers had an ample supply of wood and did erect frame structures in some parts of the state, tradition remained strong and most of their houses were of stone. The character of the stone varied from region to region, depending upon the terrain. In northeastern New Jersey, in what is now Bergen County, the houses were generally built of red sandstone hewn into neat building blocks. In what is now Morris County, puddingstone was used for walls and foundations. Limestone was frequently used in Sussex County. The houses usually faced south to catch the sun and often presented a façade that was finer than the rest of the structure. The best face was put to the road, using cut stone, while the sides and back were built of rubble or more casually cut material. In his *Military Journal of the American Revolution* James Thacher described settlements that he passed during a march through "Paramis" and "Pecquanock" from Kings Ferry: "These towns are inhabited chiefly by Dutch people. Their churches and dwelling houses are built mostly of rough stone. . . . There is a particular neatness in the appearance of their dwelling."

The gambrel roof and the flaring bell or Flemish eaves were the most conspicuous features of the style that we know as Dutch Colonial. Although these characteristics are almost always present in the early-twentieth-century versions of this style, they were rarely used in the earliest Dutch houses. These often had steep gable roofs without any overhang at all. The roof line changed over time, and by the early eighteenth century its pitch was lowered; later the familiar gambrel became common. The double slope allowed more space in the upper half-story and created the large protective overhang that contributed to the style's graceful lines and unique proportions.

The typical Dutch house had one and a half stories. The low-roofed second floor was used only for sleeping or storage and was illuminated by small gable end windows. The dormers that appear on most extant Dutch houses were later additions. A "Dutch door," divided into upper and lower sections each of which opened separately, was often used.

The Dutch built simple houses with little ornament. The uncomplicated design of the façade was broken only by windows, doors, and the front "stoep." Very few stoeps—or stoops—remain. This ancestor of the front porch was described by Peter Kalm in an account of his travels written in 1748 and 1749: "before each door there was an elevation, to which you ascend by some steps from the street; it resembled a small balcony, and had some benches on both sides on which the people sat . . . in order to enjoy the fresh aire and have the pleasure of viewing those who pass by."

*English Origins.* English settlement took place several decades after that of the Dutch. A few New Englanders found their way from the New Haven area and settled temporarily in the vicinity of Salem Creek. Other Englishmen were involved in whale hunting off Cape May. Not until 1664, however, did a significant number of English begin to establish themselves in New Jersey. Within a short time several towns were established. Middletown, Shrewsbury, Newark, Elizabethtown, Woodbridge, and Piscataway were among those that came into being with the first wave of English settlement.

Although most of the houses built during the first century of English settlement have been consumed by urban progress, isolated examples remain. Shrewsbury's Broad and Sycamore crossroads, for example, still retains much of its early character. The 1667 Allen house and its surrounding structures have changed little in two centuries. The King's Highway in Middletown is dotted with seventeenth- and eighteenth-century houses tucked into hilly woodlands. Even the larger cities have preserved and protected isolated examples of early structures.

English architecture in the colony was more diverse than that of the Dutch. Despite apparent cultural homogeneity, there were regional differences in building customs throughout England. These differences were manifested in the houses built in the colony. People from London built with brick, partly as a matter of custom and partly as a result of building codes enacted in London after the Great Fire of 1666. Settlers from rural areas often preferred to build houses using stone and continued to do so whenever possible. East Anglians, who came from an area where wood was the only available building material, had developed carpentry traditions; these, too, were continued. In the early English-built houses there is also evidence of continental building traditions that had become a part of English structural forms after earlier migrations to England from France, Germany, and Flanders. New Englanders, who arrived in substantial numbers from the north at the same time as the first English settlers, added their own architectural contributions to the already complex English architectural vocabulary. In the years that they had lived in New England they had developed their own unique forms, and some of these became elements in the New Jersey architectural landscape.

The New England Puritans had arrived in America with strong carpentry traditions, and, although stone was available, they continued to build their houses of wood. Their houses were more refined structures than those built by the Swedes. Shingles or clapboards were used for siding and wood shingles for the roof.

The kitchen lean-to at the rear was the most notable characteristic of the "New England" house. The extended roof line created by the lean-to transformed the profile of the house, altering the symmetrical silhouette to form the more dramatic saltbox. Although saltboxes from New Jersey's first century of English settlement remain, their numbers alone do not indicate the popularity of the style or the extent of the New England influence on the earlier urban landscape. Pictures of nineteenth-century New Jersey towns show street after street of New England-influenced houses. Most of the early English communities have since grown into large cities, and the early structures have been replaced by newer, larger buildings.

For many years the major English settlement was in East Jersey, where the Puritans dominated. In 1676 the Quakers acquired West Jersey and soon were building homes along the Delaware.

The Quakers followed the river north. Burlington became the capital of West Jersey in 1681. Trenton was founded at "the falls of the Delawarre" by Mahlon Stacy. Thomas Farnsworth founded Bordentown in 1682. The adventurous soon pushed inland, following the smaller rivers. Towns such as Mount Holly, founded on the shores of the Rancocas about 1700, were established along the waterways.

The brick houses that the Quakers built in the southern section of the state are the easiest of the English-built houses to recognize. These structurally uncomplicated dwellings were built in the form of a rectangle, much like brick versions of Monopoly® hotels. The only break in the façade was created by a pent roof, which formed a shallow overhang that crossed the front between the two stories. The oldest of these houses continue medieval traditions. They are tall and narrow, with steeply pitched roofs. Some are yeoman style, with random placement of windows and doors. Others are simple country versions of the English Georgian built in London near the end of the seventeenth century.

It is said that if a line were drawn from Princeton to Wilmington, Delaware, the houses north of the line would be stone and those to the south brick. This is obviously an overstatement, but "northern bricks" and "southern stones" from the first century of European settlement are not often seen. Some historians claim that the brick used in building accompanied the settlers as ballast in the holds of their ships, but facts seem to support on-site brick making as the source of these building materials.

Despite their simple silhouettes, the Quaker brick houses are often far from plain. The bricks used for the façades were frequently laid in a pattern called Flemish bond, which transformed the functional material into a form of surface ornament: instead of laying the bricks end to end in the conventional manner, the long side, or stretcher, was alternated with the short end, or header. The result is a design composed of both large and small rectangles. The surface was often enriched by using headers that had been overfired to create a glossy, steely blue; the resulting red-and-blue pattern is known as a checkerboard.

Another—and far more spectacular—brickwork effect was created by using a combination of blue headers and red stretchers to make mosaiclike patterns on the gable ends. The simplest of these designs consisted of the date of construction set in blue headers to make numbers that were over one foot high. Frequently the gable ornament also included the initials of the builder and his wife. Sometimes other designs covered the entire gable end of the house. These were often large repeated patterns composed of diamonds or zigzag lines known as diapers. In a few South Jersey houses the diaper was elaborated on and joined with other motifs, combining diamonds, ellipses, lines, dates, and initials.

Although patterned-brick houses were built in many of the colonies, New Jersey has the greatest concentration. The most and the best are to be seen in Salem County, although Mercer, Hunterdon, Gloucester, Burlington, and Cumberland counties each boast at least one. Patterned-brick houses are not easily located. They are usually found far from the main roads, often at the end of long, little-traveled country lanes that meander to the rivers. This location is not accidental. When most of these houses were new, their front doors faced the river. The pioneers who built them had to make their way inland along the water. The narrow dirt roads that now connect with the main traffic arteries were to come later. When the houses were built the river was the highway.

The easiest patterned-brick house to find is the 1734 Hancock house. Owned by the state, it is located near the center of the cluster of houses known as Hancock's Bridge. Its gable end is covered by blue and red zigzag patterns in combination with date and initials. Other houses in this part of the state are even more elaborately ornamented. On some, the dates and initials are the only decoration, while others are almost totally covered by their patterns. The most elaborate is the 1754 Dickinson house, near Alloway. Its west wall is covered with designs whose origins are attributed to English buildings dating from the sixteenth and seventeenth centuries. A complex arrangement of zigzags, solid and sprouting diamonds, and triangles, as well as initials and one of the largest dates to be seen in Salem County, create high architectural drama in a modestly scaled dwelling.

Not all the houses built by the English during their first century of settlement are as easy to identify as the patterned bricks and the salt boxes. For example, Monmouth County settlers left a legacy of early frame structures that are such subtle blends of various carpentry traditions that one must often tear down walls and examine interior structural characteristics to determine origins. Although many of the oldest houses show their age quite clearly, they do not have other strong distinguishing features.

*The Germans.* The German-influenced stone houses of Morris and Hunterdon counties are major examples of vernacular style. The first Germans arrived in New Jersey during the early years of settlement, but not until the second decade of the eighteenth century did they appear in numbers. They came mainly from Pennsylvania, determined to cross New Jersey and settle on the banks of the Hudson. According to Snell's *History of Hunterdon County*, when they crossed the Delaware River at New Hope and headed inland, "their vision was charmed with the tempting nature of the soil and the streams. They found the whole section astir with pioneers . . . they resolved to establish themselves on the good land around them." They settled in the center of Hunterdon County in a village they called Germantown. (Its name was changed to Oldwick during World War I.)

Most of the houses that the Germans built in the early 1700s were made of stone. Much like the houses they had left behind in Pennsylvania, they reflected vernacular German building traditions. Cut stone was used to build "I" houses, one room deep, with a single door, one window, and a gable and chimney—tiny structures which can still be seen close by the roadside. Gable-end windows provided light for the second floor. The abundance of stone in Hunterdon County allowed the traditional building modes to be continued without difficulty. Log construction, another traditional German form, was also used, but because of the more ephemeral nature of wood, none are known to survive.

German-built stone houses remain scattered throughout Hunterdon County and the area of Morris County that was carved from Hunterdon. Some, built into hillsides, are known as bank houses. From the road they look like conventional two-story structures, but one wall is actually a part of the slope.

Several stone houses are clustered in the western Morris County community of Long Valley. Originally called German Valley, the name was changed at about the same time that Germantown became Oldwick. The eighteenth-century houses stand close by the road in the middle of the rolling countryside that enticed the settlers to build their future in the heart of New Jersey.

Hope, situated near the towns of Liberty and Independence, was the end of a long journey for another group of Germans. These were the Moravians, an intensely devout sect, who originally came to Pennsylvania from Germany when their beliefs were no longer tolerated in their native land. They setttled in Hope around 1774. There they built stone houses in the German vernacular tradition. A cut-limestone *Gemeinhaus* (communal house) and a stone gristmill formed the nucleus of the small settlement. Clusters of houses were built of roughly cut ashlar, with brick or stone supporting the door. They were topped by steep roofs that enclosed a spacious attic. The Moravians returned to their earlier settlement in Bethlehem early in the nineteenth century, but the stone structures stand, appearing much as they did when they were built.

## Early Vernacular Styles

Early vernacular forms represent a sizable portion of the houses built during New Jersey's first hundred years. Often it is their modest scale and the patina of age that identify them; they are united by their simplicity and their direct use of materials. Small windows built with only a few panes of glass are a reminder of the limited resources of the builders. Hand-hewn wood, chinking and mortar made of earthen substances and animal hair, jumbled roof lines, and a hodgepodge of doors and windows are reminders of the first settlers' abilities to make do. The additions attached to these houses reflect growing families and the relative luxury that came with time and more sophisticated materials and tools. Although the houses are usually plain and sometimes crude, the fact that they were built at all—and their subsequent survival— confers on them an unintentional air of elegance.

# The Georgian Style

A Georgian house is easy to recognize. It presents a balanced, orderly façade. The door is always in the center, with the same number of windows on each side. This grand style reflected the increasing affluence of the colonists.

*Lawrence Township.* By the middle of the eighteenth century Georgian became the dominant form. Here, an eighteenth-century addition in the more formal Georgian style overwhelms the original seventeenth-century stone section.

*Sergeantsville*. Most of the Georgian houses built in New Jersey were simple country versions of the style. Georgian fundamentals are clearly seen, however, in the formal, symmetrical arrangement and the modest amount of classical detail. The roof line was lowered, and there was often a cornice, frequently decorated with dentils. The arched pediment could indicate a late date of construction.

*Princeton.* The windows in the Georgian house were not only larger but were made with a sash that could be raised and lowered. They were composed of many small panes and were frequently headed by a lintel that was ornamental as well as supporting. Occasionally, the larger window is found in an older house that was "modernized" during the Georgian era.

*Burlington*. The Wood Street houses, built about two hundred years ago in one of the colony's leading cities, are among the few surviving examples of an urban Georgian neighborhood.

*Lawrenceville.* An addition built after the Revolution reflects changes in style. It clearly states a post-Revolutionary construction date through its vertical character and the arched fanlight over the door.

*Mount Holly.* Many of the late Georgian houses maintained the formal symmetry of the earlier style. The pedimented dormer also remained popular. In these later houses a strong sense of the vertical was expressed in the size and shape of windows and by subtle changes in the proportions of the structural elements. In the years after the Revolution the curved arch was usually included.

During New Jersey's last decades as a colony, Georgian was the most important style. It became a part of the American architectural vocabulary through English books of architecture and carpentry that were published during the first half of the eighteenth century. William Halfpenny's *Modern Builders Assistant,* Salmon's *Palladio Londinensis,* Batty Langley's *Workingman's Treasury of Designs,* and James Gibbs's *Book of Architecture and Rules for Drawing and Several Orders* were only a few of the English "pattern books" that colonial builders used as guides. In these books were elevations, plans, and solutions to specific carpentry problems, as well as a wealth of other material. Not only did the texts offer practical instructions, they also set forth philosophical treatises about the development of taste in the new Age of Reason.

Inigo Jones (1573–1652) introduced what became known as the Georgian style to England early in the seventeenth century, drawing heavily on the works of Andrea Palladio. The style quickly became popular and was widely used in the reconstruction of London after the Great Fire of 1666. Like most English fashions of the day, it found its way across the ocean to the colonies within a few years. It quickly became the preferred style, and its popularity has never really waned. Even today the Georgian house is the dominant influence in new construction in New Jersey, as well as much of the country.

Architectural unity in the colonies began with the arrival of the Georgian style. It reflected the growth of a common culture that was beginning to overtake the diverse social and cultural practices that still connected the colonists with their European past.

A Georgian house is easy to recognize. It presents a balanced, orderly façade, the architectural expression of the ideals of the Age of Enlightenment. The rational approach meant that neither the interior layout nor the intrinsic character of the building materials was allowed to determine the design of the house. The interior layout reflected the symmetry of the exterior rather than the function of rooms.

Order was reflected in Georgian symmetry. The door was always in the center, with the same number of windows on either side. The house was two stories high, and a window above the doorway conformed with the axial nature of the house. Windows, larger than those in earlier houses, were sashed and composed of many small panes. The classic Georgian was two rooms deep. This was a new structural development in the colonies, affording more living space and allowing a grander style to serve the increasing affluence of the colonists.

Although it is easy to recognize Georgian houses, dating them often presents quite a different problem. Forever popular, these houses continued to be built long after new styles had replaced the Georgian as the latest mode. Style changes also occurred at different times in different parts of the country. In rural areas fashion changed later than in urban areas. Style moved slowly inward from the seaports to the interior and, often, from the South to the more conservative North. Even the setting of an approximate date can be complicated by the fact that the more aristocratic members of society in the newly formed United States preferred the traditional Georgian house after the Federal style had become popular with the rest of the populace. As a result, a house that might appear at first glance to date from the mid-eighteenth century could easily be one hundred years younger.

Pre-Revolutionary Georgian houses can be found in almost every part of New Jersey that was settled before the war. Although they are easily recognized as Georgians, they are frequently not pure examples of the style, including as they do elements of early settlement architecture. Building materials, roof lines, and ornaments of other cultures and other times are blended with the formality of the newer style.

# The Federal Style

As the end of the eighteenth century approached, there was a gradual shift in architectural style. The more delicate, intensely classical forms of the Federal house began to replace the orderly formality of the Georgian. But the Federal style was often tempered by the lingering architectural traditions of various settlement groups.

*Bordentown*. The elliptical arch distinguished the Federal-style doorways of late Georgian townhouses. Although the high-style Federal offered many contrasts with the earlier Georgian style, most New Jersey houses were simple country versions.

*Lawrenceville.* The elliptical fanlight was often set within a pediment. In the more refined versions of the Federal style, slender columns flanked the entry and richly carved Roman detail served as further decoration.

*Burlington.* Federal houses were characterized by flat exteriors. Elaborate detail was reserved for the interiors.

46

*Salem.* Although many Federal houses maintained the formal symmetry of the earlier Georgian, three-bay asymmetrical structures were also widely built, particularly in urban areas.

*Princeton.* The attenuated elegance of the Federal style contrasts sharply with the lines of earlier houses. Here the graceful verticality of the larger, later wing overpowers the lower section to the left, built almost a century earlier. Note that this house and many others like it continued the New Jersey tradition of lateral extensions rather than the right-angle additions typical of New England.

48 *Details.* A great deal of the exterior ornament on Federal houses can be found in doorway surrounds, as these pictures illustrate. The elliptical fanlight was frequently divided by weblike lead tracery in a variety of patterns. The pediment and narrow pilasters that often surrounded the doorway also showed classical proportions and detail.

*Princeton.* The wings of many houses form an architectural narration. Here the post-Revolutionary wing set between earlier and later sections dominates the house.

50 *Allentown/Crosswicks.* Many New Jersey villages still appear much as they did more than a century ago.

New Jersey houses provided shelter for both armies during many Revolutionary War battles. General Washington spent two winters in the Ford mansion in Morristown while his men camped in outlying fields at Jockey Hollow. He also spent considerable time at the Wallace house in nearby Somerville, and during his last days as a soldier and his first as a private citizen, he lived at Rockingham in Rocky Hill. Humbler structures quartered officers and enlisted men, although few plaques and historic markers celebrate them. Most of these houses are small, simple, and lacking in architectural distinction, but their age and, often, their role in the Revolutionary drama makes them significant, indeed, worthy of more than a casual look.

Moving events took place within the walls of many of the older houses that have survived. Thirty American soldiers were massacred, leaving bloodstains that still remain on the wooden floor of the Hancock house, a patterned-brick structure at Hancock's Bridge in Salem County. The Clark farmhouse, a simple frame dwelling at the edge of the Princeton Battlefield, sheltered General Hugh Mercer while he was dying from wounds sustained in the famous battle. In the Allen homestead in Shrewsbury, a British spy was killed, as were three Virginians who were surprised by militant Tories. Dwellings in the small village of Princeton were temporary homes for statesmen and future presidents, including Thomas Jefferson and James Madison when the Continental Congress met at Nassau Hall.

Affluence did not immediately come to postwar New Jersey; the British experienced a victory in the form of a triumphant economic counterattack. They flooded port cities with cheap English goods, and soon some of New Jersey's iron forges, furnaces, and glassworks were so deeply affected that they banked their fires and shut their doors. Alexander Hamilton attempted a defense by seeking to establish manufacturing centers, including one at the Great Falls of the Passaic River at what is now Paterson. Although the initial plan was a failure, Paterson later became one of the state's leading manufacturing cities.

There was some expansion, however, during the postwar years. Extensive improvements were made to the state's network of roads. An overland route was implemented by the construction of bridges at New Brunswick and Trenton. Privately operated toll roads called turnpikes were also developed, allowing better distribution of goods and easier travel routes, which encouraged the expansion of industry. Traffic increased and populations shifted, but this was still not enough to bring either significant growth or prosperity to New Jersey. The state did not share in the more rapid expansion of surrounding areas until developments in the nineteenth century provided a more fertile setting for industry.

New Jersey's lack of prosperity was reflected in the houses that were built in the first decades of the republic. Those who were able to build grand houses were usually drawn to the more cosmopolitan life across the rivers in New York and Philadelphia. In New Jersey there was little, if any, high-style construction. Instead, the new houses were mainly vernacular blends of current and recent styles that frequently reflected the earlier settlement forms.

The major style was still the Georgian. Houses continued to be built using the formal balances and ordered lines that were characteristic of that style. Georgian, however, was not the only style. Settlement traditions persisted and were evident in materials and details. The Germans continued their use of masonry construction. The Dutch still used fine-cut stone for house fronts and less elegant rubble for side walls. In the north the Dutch frequently built the gambrel-roofed houses of earlier years. Throughout the state there were also unique dwellings that represented a point in time rather than a specific style. Often a response to need, they were without adornment and, frequently, without formal plan.

As the end of the eighteenth century approached, there was a gradual shift in architectural style. Excavations at Pompeii and other classical sites caught the imagination of English architects, among them the Adam brothers. Robert Adam (1728–1792) was the most influential and best-known British architect of this era. The exterior and interior structural vocabulary based upon newly discovered and popular classical elements that he developed quickly became the dominant architectural fashion. The more delicate, intensely classical forms of the Federal house began to replace the orderly formality of the Georgian and further refine residual settlement patterns.

In the United States the Adam style was known as Federal in celebration of the era during which it first became popular. The new republic eschewed the Englishness of the Adam name and, in the United States, the books of William and James Pain, among others, shaped the style. The extreme popularity of the Federal style was based on the belief that it was appropriate for citizens of the new American democracy, particularly for members of the emerging, newly affluent mercantile class. The Georgian house, however, remained popular among the more aristocratic, although this division of house style by social class, like most architectural distinctions, can not be rigidly applied. Many structures, known today as post-Georgian, were built at the same time as those called Federal. Despite the new label, these were essentially the same as the earlier Georgians. The lingering Georgian mode reflected not only personal conservatism but political sentiment and, often, the time it took for the new style to travel from more sophisticated coastal cities to inland areas.

Although the shift to Federal was taking place throughout the nation, the difficulties of communication and the manner in which style moved from one area to another led to evolution rather than precipitous change. New fashions and the resultant transition to the Federal style reached most of the country via travelers' reports or books of architecture. This information frequently arrived piecemeal; changes occurred one at a time, in the shape of the window, design of the doorway or dormer or the selection of new forms of ornament.

Often, the Federal house did not represent a radical change from the Georgian form. In many city houses, Georgian symmetry was replaced by an asymmetrical façade in which the door was placed to one side. Elsewhere, the Georgian design evolved into the Federal through subtle alterations in proportion and through the addition and alteration of details without major structural changes. The shift from the appearance of solidity to delicacy and lightness was the most significant difference. The squareness of the Georgian house was softened by the introduction of curving forms, small oval windows, and round-arched dormers, as well as a variety of classically inspired ornament, including elliptical and geometric decorations. Fanlights became semicircular. They were made of leaded glass arranged in delicate patterns that often included finely wrought metal sculptural ornament as part of the design. In high-style houses, festoons, garlands, and arched recesses and bays were used to alter Georgian proportions and to lighten the structures' more severe character.

A feeling of verticality characterized the Federal design. Pilasters or columns were much more slender and graceful than those used for earlier structures. Supports were widely spaced on porches to contribute to the sense of lightness. Occasionally balustrades were added at the top of a house to mask the roof line and to continue the illlusion of airiness.

Federal houses in New Jersey were more often architectural blends than examples of high style. Most that were built in the cities, which may have been grand, have long since been replaced. Those that remain are usually in areas where fashion came late and factors other than current style were influential. The Federal design was often tempered by the lingering architectural traditions of various settlement groups, traditions which remained important until the beginning of the nineteenth century. When new design elements arrived they did not signify the end of older forms, but rather were incorporated into them. As a result, many New Jersey Federal houses could still be considered a form of settlement architecture. Examples can be seen in fieldstone post-Georgian houses with arched fanlights and elliptical windows, arched dormers, and slender columns on either side of the door. Paired end chimneys connected by a bridge of brick, another characteristic of the Federal style, often marry earlier brick traditions with the later mode.

In the more fashionable urban areas, particularly in the southern part of the state, good brick Federals still stand. Their graceful arched entryways and delicate fanlights are unmistakable. Mount Holly, Bordentown, Moorestown, and Burlington are among the many towns with good vernacular versions of this style.

The frame Federals built farther north share the arched fanlights and dormers as well as entryways embellished with slender pilasters and classical ornament. These houses often resemble Georgians and are not easy to distinguish from the earlier style. The arch is usually the hallmark of the Federal, particularly when used over the doorway or in dormers.

Federal details also made a bridge to the style that followed. The transition can be seen in many nineteenth-century houses where the presence of a lacy, arched fanlight marks the entrance of a house whose other details clearly mark it Greek Revival, the first style to sweep the nation.

# Greek Revival

No other style was quite so widely accepted as the Greek Revival. The classical architectural vocabulary was used in some form on many of even the simplest vernacular houses built between 1836 and 1850. Endless combinations of pediments, cornices, and columns surrounded doors and windows and topped walls, determining the character of the American house for nearly two decades.

*Belle Meade.* As always, older styles persisted in rural areas. One of the simplest expressions of the Greek syntax was the classically inspired doorway, often found on a house that had remained essentially Georgian in form.

*New Brunswick.* In some Greek Revival houses the classical lines of the temple were reproduced quite faithfully, from the design of the capitals to the proportions of the colossal portico. A semicircular window called a lunette was sometimes included within the pediment to provide attic illumination.

*Freehold*. The term *Greek* was often too specific. Occasionally, a modicum of Roman influence could be found in the sparser temple-form house.

*Princeton.* Most "Grecian" houses were loose interpretations of the classical forms. Some were blends that included elements of older fashions such as the Federal elliptical fanlight and later details such as a bracketed Italianate porch. The overall effect was the popular local image of "Greek Revival."

*Princeton.* Although some of these houses include structural allusions to other styles, the rows of Steadman-designed houses on Alexander Street represent an unusual concentration of richly detailed vernacular versions of "Grecian architecture." The façades of these houses are essentially similar, but the variety and quality of the detail establish the character of each dwelling.

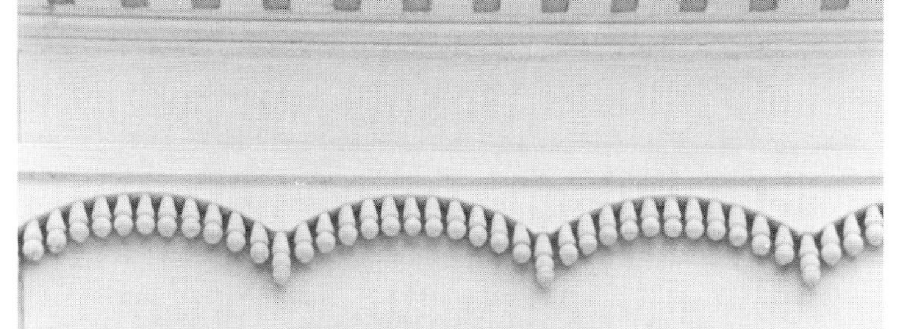

*Details.* Ornament was as important as silhouette on the Greek Revival house. Although the trim always made reference to the classical architectural syntax, builders often applied these motifs in a creative and individualistic manner.

*Flemington*. The Greek Revival house provided an opportunity for rich combinations of ornament. Robust foliate forms can be found on some of the finer dwellings. Decorative window units in the form of grille-covered openings in the frieze were occasionally used to admit light to the attic without creating the illusion of height.

*Flemington.* A hint of the Victorian concern with more romantic architectural forms occasionally invaded the restrained lines and softened the rigid geometry of the Greek Revival.

*Mount Holly.* Often the Greek influence was only part of a wealth of architectural details. This row of masonry houses built before the middle of the nineteenth century boasts elliptical fanlights, brick corner quoins, an elaborate archway, and a bracketed porch with a Tuscan air, as well as the Greek Revival doorway, classically oriented pediment, and Ionic columns.

Prosperity continued to bypass New Jersey during the early nineteenth century. Manufacturing had been hurt after the war and, much as they do today, New Jersey's two dynamic neighbors, New York City and Philadelphia, attracted most of the capital necessary for growth. A great deal of the state's commercial activity was in the form of traffic through the corridor. Turnpikes were developed as a major form of private enterprise, connecting the rich markets across the two rivers, but the network of roads soon turned to "hopeless ruts and quagmires" beneath the wheels of wagons carrying grain, passengers, and goods.

John Stevens was one of the first to attempt to solve the transportation dilemma. He struggled with the legislature for years in order to develop a railroad, but by the time it was in service it was only one of several new transportation enterprises. By the mid-1830s coal and iron were being hauled over the mountains from the Delaware to the Hudson through the Morris Canal, using an elaborate series of locks, inclined planes, and channels. The Delaware and Raritan Canal linked Bordentown, Trenton, Princeton, and New Brunswick; and within a few years several railroads served New Jersey. Manufacturing that had been limited to local markets could now serve other parts of the country. Factory towns formed around the growing industries. Concentrations of small houses and inns, many of which still remain, grew up along the canals. The arrival of the railroad was the occasion for small villages to begin the process of becoming cities.

Although New Jersey was about to enter a period of great expansion, it was not yet a rich or sophisticated state, and its architecture continued to reflect the moderate circumstances of its people. Most houses built during the early decades of the nineteenth century were conservative in appearance and modest in size. There were intimations of the delightful discovery that architects and carpenters would soon make of the classical architectural styles, but these appeared only as occasional elements within more traditional structural forms.

Classical design elements had been part of the Georgian and Federal styles. The Georgian originally grew out of the work of Palladio, a sixteenth-century Italian architect. All but the simplest versions were adorned with some manner of column, molding, or ornament inspired by the ancient Greek or Roman architectural vocabulary. Federal houses were even more closely joined with classical forms through the columns, arches, and ellipses that were an integral part of their design.

Although Roman-style houses were occasionally built during the early years of the nineteenth century, the style was not readily accepted by architects or the general public. It was felt that association with both the Roman Empire and the Emperor Napoleon cast an ideological shadow over the clean lines of the Roman house.

There were no philosophical or political ambiguities associated with the Greek style. "Grecian architecture," as it was called, had neither the connections with empire nor the association with contemporary political conflict that were tied to the Roman concept. Instead, it was thought to reflect the ideals of the new republic. It inspired images of democracy, liberty, and the lofty philosophy and culture that characterized Greek society during its noblest days. Not only Greek architecture but the names of new towns such as Sparta and Adelphia, instead of the Salems and New Providences of an earlier era, illustrated the wide acceptance of this association.

Elements of Greek architecture can be found in Philadelphia builders' manuals as early as the late eighteenth century, but not until the 1820s did it sweep the nation as the architecture of preference. Grecian architecture was welcomed at all levels of society, and its syntax became the basis for a new American architectural vocabulary. In describing how well the Greek idiom adapted to American needs, Talbot Hamlin stated in *Greek Revival Architecture in America* that "the new country demanded a new, American, architecture. The country's needs were her own, her materials were peculiarly hers. . . . There is hardly an architect of the first water in this nineteenth century America who does not . . . strive to design buildings of a new type—not copies of ancient buildings but American buildings, only the details of which were inspired by the classic."

No other style was ever so universally accepted as Greek Revival. In almost every village and city in the eastern half of the United States, "Main Street" includes at least one imposing Greek temple in marble, granite, local stone, or wood, appropriately fitted out with columns, topped with one or a blend of orders, pediment, and entablature. In New Jersey, as elsewhere, most such classical re-creations were built as churches, banks, courthouses, theaters, and athenea, although domestic examples exist. Smaller, less imposing, and often less architecturally pure versions of these grand structures are usually found along side streets and byways.

Greek Revival was the first popular American style that did not draw heavily on English architectural thinking. Although there was great interest in classical architecture in England at the same time, the books and carpenters' guides used here were written by Americans for their countrymen, and, for the first time, architecture in the United States was not determined by the tastes and preferences of people across the ocean.

The style's popularity was reflected in the number and variety of carpenters' and builders' guides that encouraged the uses of Greek-inspired forms. The books led in turn to even more houses in the same mode. Minard Lafever's *Young Builders' General Instructor* was published in Newark in 1829. Other influential American publications, such as Asher Benjamin's *American Builders' Companion* (1826), *Builders' Guide* (1839), and *Practical House Carpenter* (1830), and John Haviland's *Builders' Assistant* (three volumes, 1818–1821), made it possible for builders and carpenters everywhere to build Greek houses for their customers.

Although the temple form is the one most readily associated with Greek architecture, most of the Greek Revival houses built in New Jersey were more modest in nature. Houses with a hint of pediment, pilasters rather than columns, and some unobtrusive ornament are familiar. These houses rarely have dramatic impact, but they are undisputably Greek in origin. In rural areas the houses are frequently built in the traditional Georgian or mid-Atlantic farmhouse style but have Grecian trim, doorways, and porticoes. In the towns the houses are frequently three-bayed, with flat or low roofs, a modest amount of Greek ornament, and some form of Greek-inspired entryway. Many Greek Revival elements are similar enough to those used in the Georgian and Federal modes to make identification of vernacular Greek Revival difficult at times.

There is no such ambiguity about high-style Grecian architecture. The most notable characteristic of these houses is their resemblance to the classical temple. Unlike earlier structures, high-style Greek Revival houses are sited so that the roof edge runs from front to back, presenting the gable end to the street and converting the gable's appearance into that of a pediment, which in turn sits upon an entablature constructed in the classical manner. This is supported by several columns topped with one of the formal orders or else with an ornament created by blending Ionic and Corinthian designs.

In both high-style and vernacular examples, the curvilinear forms characteristic of the Federal style were replaced by the strong, simple lines of the rectangle. Arches and ellipses had decorated earlier houses. Greek keys and dentils now replaced the garlands in the friezes. Doorways were topped by oblong multi-paned transoms and simple sidelights. Where there is no pediment the Greek Revival house is generally a cube or rectangle without any visible slope to the roof. The columns are the most conspicuous characteristic of this form of Greek Revival, and they dominate the façade. In some houses the simplified lines of this style were used as a setting for elaborate iron detail, including ornate grilles set within the friezes, an ornament composed of foliate forms as well as geometric motifs.

Greek Revival houses were usually designed by builder-architects. There was not yet any formal school of architecture in the United States, and the men who shaped the houses at this time often began their careers as carpenters' apprentices. Those who were able ultimately surfaced to perform the architect's function. In Princeton, Charles Steadman (1790–1868) built a great many Greek Revival houses that are outstanding for their proportions and the quality and richness of their detail. Working most actively from 1825 to 1845, he eschewed the temple form and, instead, built simpler versions of the Greek Revival style. Many good Steadman houses exist in the Princeton area; Alexander Street presents an unbroken row of these fine dwellings, an unusual architectural phenomenon. So many houses in close proximity provide an opportunity to consider the variety and combination of detail—porches, entryways, and cornices, for example—that existed within the formal limitations of the style.

In Flemington, on Main Street, several houses designed by Mahlon Fisher present a quite different version of the Greek Revival house. Again, there are no pediments, but the majesty of the columns and the drama created by the scale of the structures and their combinations of ornament make these houses out of the ordinary. Window surrounds on these houses are ornate and combine elements more often seen on later structures. Some of the ornament is painted in contrasting colors, accenting the classic lines and the elegant detail. Although the details are remarkable, it is their clean rectangular form that determines the character of these richly decorated houses.

By the middle of the nineteenth century, Grecian architecture was no longer considered high style. Vernacular versions continued to be built in outlying areas well into the 1850s, but fashion turned its back on the classical mode. The people who set the style decided it was "foreign" and not suited to the needs of the country. The almost instant wealth that the Industrial Revolution produced created a need for more ostentatious consumption, and this was reflected in the houses that were built in New Jersey as the second half of the nineteenth century began.

# Romantic Victorians

By mid-century the Greek Revival had all but disappeared as a fashionable style, and Gothic became the architecture of preference because of both its romantic associations and its lofty Christian connections.

*Lawrence Township.* Exterior variety was the dominant characteristic of the Gothic house. While the pointed-arch window was the hallmark, it was often only one of many architectural elements. As in this house, it was usually accompanied by bays, clusters of windows, wall dormers, and other kinds of arches. More complex dwellings even had little round windows. The façade was often an intricate arrangement of wall gables, projections, and generally irregular features, all of which satisfied the Victorian desire for the picturesque.

*Mount Holly.* In its grandest manifestations—of which this brick creation is an example—the Gothic house became an intricate tapestry of bays, porches, wall gables, and dormers. Wooden trim suggesting Gothic tracery embroidered the edges of steeply pitched roofs and gables, which were then topped with finials. Port cochères like this one were another common feature of larger Gothic dwellings.

*Lawrenceville*. The cross-gable, neatly dividing the roof in the front of the house, was a common feature of the vernacular Gothic dwelling. Details receive a good deal of attention, even in the simplest Gothic house. Eared drip moldings often topped windows that were designed with wooden tracerylike details. Tall, clustered chimneys were built in imaginative shapes, adding additional visual activity to an already busy roof.

*Mount Holly.* In his pattern books, Downing encouraged the use of board-and-batten siding for Gothic cottages. The vertical lines created by this type of exterior intensified the sense of upward movement considered an essential characteristic of the Gothic house.

*Details.* Elaborate pointed or arched windows were perhaps the most constant hallmark of the Gothic style, whether high style or vernacular.

*Moorestown.* As time passed the Gothic house became more massive and coarse. The character of the ornament changed, and occasionally the aspiring verticality of the style was expressed by little more than the steep pitch of the roofs, gables, and dormers.

*Plainfield*. Wooden Gothic houses took many forms. Some depended upon roof line or window shape for their connection with the style. Others represented an effort to duplicate masonry effects in wood; it was in this way that the term Carpenter Gothic originated.

*Cape May City*. The carpenter's art often lent a churchlike air to the frame house. Even the unlikely mansard that tops the tower of this dwelling does not interfere with the ecclesiastical solemnity of the pointed windows and important arched entrance.

*Flemington.* The carpenter's fancy soon removed the wooden house from the realm of formal Gothic. Instead, the house often became a foil for a flourish of wooden ornament that seemed the product of whimsey as much as historical influence. In place of historically correct quatrefoils and tracery, roof lines and porches were embroidered with a seemingly unlimited assortment of icicles, curlicues, and flowery trim.

*Blairstown/Cape May.* The formal contour of the Roman arch was often converted into a lacy confection whose appearance carried hardly a hint of its more austere beginnings. Although much ingeniously designed ornament has fallen victim to time and practical concerns, enough survives to allow us some share of this nineteenth-century form of folk art.

*Details.* Dormers and gables were seldom left unadorned. Instead, fretwork and filigree distinguished their appearance and converted them into romantic bowers.

*Ocean Grove.* Ocean Grove has retained more of its Victorian air than most New Jersey towns. Begun as a religious retreat, the community continues to resist worldly influence and preserve its original appearance, which is characterized by the rich ornamentation that survives on balconies, porches, and vergeboards.

*Ocean Grove*. This unique seaside community offers more than one way to escape from the complexities of the late twentieth century. Victorian residential forms include not only gingerbread cottages but a summer tent community, in use for a century.

*Princeton*. This elegant villa with a decidedly ecclesiastical air, built before mid-century, is one of the few Gothic houses in the state that approach high style. As preceding pages illustrate, most New Jersey gothics were vernacular interpretations.

Victoria was queen of England from 1837 to 1901. During the sixty-four years that she ruled the British Empire, the Industrial Revolution and the accompanying new technology changed the lives of both rich and poor in the Old and the New Worlds. In the United States an agrarian country was transformed into a nation of manufacturers and city dwellers. Not only were there new kinds of goods and new means of travel, but there were also new rich, new poor, and, ultimately, a new middle class that grew to dominate American society.

During the nineteenth century, changes in the social structure, shifts in popular taste, and the development of new technologies generated complex changes in the nature of the American home. A new wealthy class craved ostentation. Emerging industrial cities created a need for cheaply built, easily constructed houses. More efficient systems of transportation, covering a wider geographic base, increased opportunities for expansion. As a result, the appearance, location, and character of the family dwelling changed radically. A variety of architectural styles became available to an eager public.

Not long ago, the "Victorian" label had pejorative connotations. In a social context it symbolized prudery and hypocrisy. Inside the house it was a synonym for the heavy, dark, cluttered, and ornate, bringing to mind beaded curtains, flocked wallpaper, fringed lampshades, and lion's claws on everything. Architecturally it evoked buildings that were often too large and eccentrically designed, with an overabundance of ornament.

Time has provided sufficient perspective to allow a change of sentiment. Former architectural ugly ducklings are now appreciated as expressions of their time and enjoyed for their joyous structural abandon. Ornament, once considered extraneous and frequently removed from houses in "improvement" efforts, is now appreciated for its sculptural quality and architectural effect as well as its historical significance. The picturesque silhouette, previously rejected by many modernists for practical as well as aesthetic reasons, is currently enjoyed for the variety it contributes to the landscape and for its merit as a design form.

Good examples of Victorian style are easy to find in New Jersey, in large part because the state experienced much of its growth and development when Victorian architecture was thriving. Entire villages and small cities still retain their nineteenth-century aspect. Commercial structures, hotels, banks, and public buildings that have remained essentially unchanged for a century set the stage for present-day life in towns such as Newton, Clinton, Hackettstown, Belvidere, Bordentown, and Bridgeton.

The complex series of railroads and canals that were developing during the first part of the nineteenth century facilitated New Jersey's rapid growth. Improved transportation meant the availability of coal via train and canal boat, marking the end of dependence on the water wheel as the major source of power. Coal for power allowed the construction of increasingly larger factories wherever there were transportation routes.

Enticed by increased employment opportunities provided by new factories, people came to New Jersey from other states or, if they were natives, remained to work in the state. They left their farms and headed for rapidly growing industrial centers like Paterson, Trenton, Newark, Camden, and Woodbridge.

Natural resources determined much of the development. An underground network of rich veins of clay permitted the growth of the great potteries in Trenton and Flemington and brick manufacturing in the New Brunswick area. The excellent supply of fine sand in the southern part of the state led to the large-scale manufacture of glass, for which New Jersey became famous. Steel, beer, fabric, and hundreds of previously rare or costly items that had suddenly become necessities were made in New Jersey and shipped to markets all over America.

New Jersey's population doubled between 1830 and 1860, generating an increased need for additional housing and changing the face of the state. Workers' houses were built in large numbers, close to the factories. Affluent owners and managers also chose to live nearby. Villages that began as factory towns were soon bustling cities. Small but densely populated New Jersey became the fifth most important manufacturing state by 1880, the same year that the census bureau first described New Jersey as "urban."

## Suburban Genesis

Industrial development was only one of several factors in New Jersey's growth. The increasingly easy trip to and from New York created another type of new resident. Vacationers escaped from the summer heat of the city to the deep woods at Schooley's Mountain, the hills of Plainfield, and the quiet countryside around Shrewsbury. Bayonne, accessible by ferry, was called the Newport of New York and was the site of now vanished estates that offered their owners cool harbor breezes and a view of sailing ships crossing New York Bay. People from Camden made the trip to the "healthful" seaside at Cape May by ferry in two days; Long Branch, more conveniently located along the railroad, quickly grew to rival the famous Cape as a seaside resort. Elegant "cottages" and enormous villas were built along the dunes to capture the cool air on porches and verandas. As soon as the railroad linked the northwestern section of the state with the more populous areas, the Ramapo Mountains, too, began to attract vacationers, and Greenwood Lake and its surrounding hills and valleys also developed as a resort area.

The lure of trees, fresh air, and other joys of country living proved too great to resist. Many of the vacationers from the cities soon became commuters. After the Civil War, towns that were on the railroad rapidly became Wall Street suburbs. Bankers and brokers built houses reflecting their own sense of grandeur and importance. Winding lanes were cut into the hillsides of Plainfield and Montclair to lead to the homes of men who earned their living across the river. A train called the Morristown Bankers' Express, scheduled to coincide with the shorter hours of the upper-echelon banker's day, rushed its passengers to and from Hoboken, where they could cross to New York by ferry and return in mid-afternoon.

The value of living in the countryside was popularized in books that offered both advice on how to "improve" the landscape and a selection of dwelling styles. Villages, virgin woodlands, and acres of farmlands soon became landscaped byways and manicured lawns that could provide the "natural" setting so important for the good Victorian life. These rolling lawns were the site of many enormous houses built in the variety of architectural poses considered suitable for a nineteenth-century family of substance.

Victorian reverence for nature combined with promotions by the railroads and real estate developers to attract an ever-widening range of people from the city to the more healthful and bucolic farmland of Bergen County. Bergen Fields, originally the Dutch town of Schrallenburgh, advertised itself, citing "22 trains daily . . . Commutation 10 cents . . . TERMS: $10 a lot down on day of sale." Soon more modest houses built by people of moderate means joined the imposing structures that were filling in the open countryside.

## Technological Developments

Without the new building technology it would not have been possible for the state to grow as fast as it did. Inexpensive machine-made nails replaced more expensive hand-forged spikes. Improved sawmill machinery permitted the production of standardized lumber. The introduction of the balloon frame in the 1830s was probably the single most significant development. This new means of framing, which gained wide acceptance by mid-century, simplified the construction of the supporting structure of the house. Costly and complex mortise-and-tenon joints were replaced by a simpler method of framing in which the sidewalls were constructed of two-by-four studs. Using this method of construction, two relatively untrained men could do work that had previously required the skills of several trained artisans.

New technology did more than change structural procedures. The invention of the steam-powered scroll saw radically affected the exterior of one house. Ornaments, which had previously been the product of laborious handcrafting, could now be rapidly executed by the less skilled carpenter with the aid of a machine. As a result, standardized builders' supplies became available for the first time. Thanks to lower construction costs, even the most modest houses could be planned with some form of gingerbread, icicles, or decorated window trim, in the manner of more expensive dwellings.

## Transition

The beginning of the Victorian era marked the decline in popularity of the Greek Revival. Although its demise took longer in rural areas, by the 1850s Grecian architecture was almost universally rejected for more up-to-date styles. This also marked the end of the era when just one style was popular at any given time. Instead of the orderly architectural progression from Colonial to Georgian to Federal to Greek, house fashion was now subject to a myriad of influences. People could choose between Gothic, Italianate, and Egyptian styles and still be in fashion.

The character of the new architectural choices and the rejection of the classical style reflected strong national interest in romantic themes. People eagerly read the works of Byron, Scott, (particularly *Ivanhoe*), and Walpole, hoping, as Walpole had written, to have the satisfaction "of imprinting the gloom of abbeys and cathedrals" on their own homes. The political and philosophical ideals that people had ascribed to building styles were now replaced by the desire for residences that created an appropriate mood.

The house also became an important expression of status at this time. New wealth, often rapidly acquired, was accompanied by the ambition to own a dwelling that would reassure its inhabitants of their importance and convince those who saw it that it was the home of powerful, prosperous people.

## Architects, Builders, and Pattern Books

During these years the role of the architect became more important in the design of domestic architecture, although there was still little in the way of formal training to be had in the United States. It was not until 1863 that the first architects were formally educated (at the Massachusetts Institute of Technology). Prior to that, architects were usually self-trained, or else learned as apprentices. A few, like Ithiel Town (1782–1844), Benjamin Henry Latrobe (1764–1820), Robert Mills (1781–1855), and Alexander Jackson Davis (1803–1892), became influential, however, and their designs determined much of the appearance of nineteenth-century America.

Some of the best-known American house designers of the period were responsible for residences in New Jersey. John Notman (1810–1865) was the architect for Riverside, one of the first Italianate houses in America, built for Bishop Doane in Burlington in the late 1830s. Another Notman Italianate stands in Bordentown, and several important examples of his work can be found in Princeton. In Mount Holly, he created a "unique semi-Oriental cottage" that received national attention when Andrew Jackson Downing described it in his famous *Treatise on Landscape Gardening*. Alexander Jackson Davis, possibly the most influential architect of this time, designed Llewellyn Park in West Orange in the 1850s and 1860s. The collection of Gothic houses that originally constituted Llewellyn Park was, in fact, one of the earliest subdivisions and was cited in almost every house book written at that time. The streets and houses of this "garden suburb," all designed by one individual, were in a sense the conceptual ancestors of today's sprawling Levittowns and planned communities.

Most of the Victorian houses in New Jersey, however, were at least one step removed from high-style, architect-designed structures. Their appearance was shaped by the plans and instructions in popular books of house design known as pattern books. An increasing number of publications offered guidance on a variety of subjects, including dress, manners, and the suitable appearance of dwellings. Prospective owners, carpenters, and builders found advice on how to plan and build houses, and often how to finish and furnish them as well. Drawings, floor plans, and structural data brought elements of high-style architecture within the reach of the middle class.

The most influential of the early pattern books were those of Andrew Jackson Downing (1815–1852). Carpenters and builders throughout the nation built houses based on drawings and plans in his *Cottage Residences* (1842) and *The Architecture of Country Houses* (1850). Downing, who had been trained as a landscape architect, assembled the work of other architects and provided a text offering information on everything the prospective owner or builder might need. Not only house styles but philosophical rationales for design and material selection as well as discourses on "the real meaning of architecture" were included in Downing's copious texts.

He told his readers what a farmhouse should be, defined the cottage, and offered a selection of villas and country houses which he connected with "deeper" meanings and pithy views of American society, including "the true meaning of the American home."

Downing strongly advocated the irregular silhouette of the picturesque and was influential in making it the dominant characteristic of the Victorian house. He described the picturesque as depending "upon the opposite conditions of matter-irregularity and a partial want of proportion and symmetry." He stated, "It necessarily follows that all architecture in which beauty of expression strongly predominates over pure material beauty must be more or less picturesque." And, if these values were not enough to discourage his readers from continued appreciation of the "unpicturesque" Greek houses, he described the pediment of the temple cottage as having "not the least utility . . . too high for shade . . . and . . . entirely destitute of truthfulness."

Having once established the climate for change in the architectural scene, Downing and his contemporaries presented the public with the means for achieving a proper dwelling. The less affluent could select from a variety of cottages including a "workingman's model" of a Gothic cottage, or similar modest styles that were either bracketed, Swiss, Tuscan (or Italianate). Those fortunate enough to be able to build a villa had an even more complex array of designs from which to choose. It was possible to build a villa in English rural style, rural Gothic Italian, Romanesque Norman, Anglo-Italian, as well as other regional interpretations.

Although the pattern books seemingly offered a variety of architectural riches, there were only two major styles. Most houses built during the early Victorian years were either some form of the Gothic or else a version of the Italian, or Tuscan, style. Gothic architecture became popular because of its connection with Romantic literature, its picturesque silhouette, its association with the virtues of Christianity, and the belief that it looked "natural" in the landscape. Italianate houses, whose flat-topped towers and asymmetrically grouped round-arched windows easily conformed to popular standards of taste, soon became the second major style.

The other revival styles built at this time were of minor significance. Only one other became at all noteworthy in New Jersey. This was the Egyptian revival, originally popularized in France after Napoleon's campaign on the Nile. This truly exotic style was adapted for the gates of the old state prison in Trenton and the courthouse in Newark; it was never widely used in residential architecture, although occasional elements of the style can be seen in churches and dwellings.

## Gothic Revival

Although elements of Gothic design first appeared in this country in the works of Batty Langley in the eighteenth century, and occasional Gothic details were included in much earlier structures, the style was little used until the 1830s. It was initially popularized by Alexander Jackson Davis, then a partner in the influential firm of Town and Davis, which made standardized Gothic plans available for small sums. It was first given widespread exposure, however, in Downing's pattern books. Some version of the Gothic house was available to meet every aspect of the enormous popular demand.

Gothic forms lent themselves readily to ecclesiastical function. The Gothic used in private dwellings was usually a less elaborate version of this style. The pointed arch, which was the engineering keystone upon which the original style rested, remained the dominant characteristic of the nineteenth-century versions. Ornamental bargeboards, wall dormers, off-center towers, and leaded glass were frequently used elements in the Gothic house. The interpretations of Gothic were so diverse, however, that houses in this category might include only one or a combination of the style's characteristic details.

There are relatively few high-style Gothic houses in New Jersey. The combination, number, and quality of historically appropriate details in those that do exist distinguish them from their vernacular equivalents. One can easily share the self-satisfaction of the owners of such houses as Ashurst in Mount Holly and the John B. McCready House in Cape May. Each time they approached their ponderous towers and looked up at steep gables topped by finials that seemed to reach for the heavens, they must have felt gratified to share in the lofty importance of these dwellings.

Less elaborate, less dramatic versions of Gothic can be seen in numerous smaller frame and masonry versions of the style. They range from small but strongly vertical structures with a single pointed dormer or gable window to the carpenters' extravaganzas that lost sight of the dignity that characterized the original Gothic and were instead bouquets of wooden ornament made up of exuberant curlicues and spiky finials and spindles.

Between the two extremes are innumerable versions of this style. Many have board-and-batten siding, a building method encouraged by Downing that continued the vertical movement essential to the style. Others are built of stone or clapboard. Some look very like the pattern book originals and include much that is authentically Gothic, while others accommodate popular fashion to individual preference.

New Jersey is rich in wooden versions of the Gothic style. Although much of the gingerbread trim has been removed over the years as a concession to convenience and "modernization," a good deal still remains. Wooden interpretations of masonry forms, generally known as Carpenter Gothic, abound. Gloriously complex porches and vergeboards still enrich the appearance of villages in the northwestern and southwestern sections of the state. Even more wait to be discovered on back roads.

Cape May's Gothic houses include the famous gingerbread-trimmed Pink House. Cape May Point, a less architecturally dramatic nineteenth-century neighbor, has simpler but still excellent examples of the style. One of the most charming of New Jersey's nineteenth-century gingerbread villages is Ocean Grove. It has successfully resisted almost all twentieth-century incursions, although asbestos shingle has experienced a minor triumph there. Ocean Grove is later than most Carpenter Gothic, but tiny houses on small lots present a splendid, dense array of the carpenter's fancy, and hint of pattern book originals. The same Victorian variety and charm can be found in Island Heights, another summer resort originally founded as a religious retreat. Here, tiny Victorian summer cottages are tucked into wooded hills along the Toms River.

These are only a few of the many communities in the state that were shaped by the nineteenth-century carpenter's saw and the far-reaching influence of the early cathedral forms. Indeed, the profusion of cottages and villas that remain is such that it appears there was a Gothic house for almost everyone.

## Italianate

Together with the Gothic, the Italianate influence shaped most domestic architecture during the early Victorian era. Italianate was almost as popular as Gothic, and examples of the style can be seen in New Jersey towns that developed just before the Civil War.

Again, there were choices within the style. Downing provided his readers with a "suburban cottage" and a grander "villa," both in the Italian style, as well as an Anglo-Italian villa for those who could not make the full architectural commitment. A frame version of the style, found in Freehold, closely resembles a plate from his *Cottage Residences.* Downing distinguished between the villa and the smaller house, stating, "A cottage is a dwelling so small that the household duties may all be performed by the family, or with the assistance of not more than one or two domestics; a villa is a country house requiring the care of at least three servants."

The villa, with its high, square tower, round-arched windows, and studied asymmetry satisfied the desire for the "picturesque." Its eccentricities of silhouette and the asymmetrical façade created by the variety of window groupings allowed the Italianate house, like the Gothic, to sit naturally in the landscape and create a harmonious vista. Conspicuous brackets under the roof, and balconies and porches, often called loggias or piazzas, completed the house. Villas were usually frame or stucco. One of the most beautiful examples—Bishop house—stands on Rutgers University's New Brunswick campus.

A less dramatic but equally popular Italian-influenced style, inspired by the Renaissance palazzo, was built at the same time as the more elaborate villa. Referred to by some historians as Italianate, or Cube Italian, it was sheltered by a low roof whose large overhang was supported by brackets. The roof was often topped by a central cupola or belvedere that provided a view of the countryside. In order to satisfy popular demand for ornament, the belvedere was often adorned by large elaborate finials. A front porch extended across the width of the house and usually carried its share of carved and sawed decorations, interrupting the sense of mass that was created by the simple cubic form.

Houses that appear to be a compromise between the more and less elaborate forms are often concentrated in the urbanized areas of towns like Plainfield, where relatively smaller lots made the true villa difficult to build. Here, three-story towers top houses that are clearly Tuscan yet do not ramble like the villas.

The Italianate style continued to flourish in the post–Civil War years. Much of New Jersey's Italianate architecture consists of the simple versions of the style that were carpenters' interpretations of pattern books, and the style's essentially plain character left room for all kinds of creative trimwork. Roman-arched windows were often translated into French by the elaborate character of their hoodmolds. Heavy cornices and moldings were occasionally used to convert the attractive balances into more ponderous spatial relationships. Paired roof brackets, too, became part of the style. The earlier simplicity of the villa disappeared.

The Cube Italian house also retained its popularity. Although originally conceived as an uncomplicated form, it, too, lost its simplicity and became a foil for luxurious ornament. Tall parlor windows, often elaborately trimmed, looked out on porches embellished with equal abandon. The stylistic conversion was completed by the paired brackets that ultimately gave the style another name. Known as the American Bracketed Villa, it became widely popular.

Early Victorian houses—both the Gothic and Italianate—were more clearly defined, stylistically, than the complex architectural combinations that were to follow. Yet the patterns and directions used to build them allowed more flexibility than do today's blueprints and served as a base for the skill of the builder. Each bargeboard, bracket, and finial remained as unique as those who designed and crafted them.

# High Victorian Variety

The irregular silhouette of the Italian villa easily satisfied the Victorian desire for the picturesque. The style was prominently featured in pattern books. Downing praised it, remarking upon the "satisfaction derived from harmony growing out of variety," which he compared to a Beethoven symphony. It was this variety, too, that made the Italianate the style of transition between the historically inspired lines of the early Victorian house and the more complex and flamboyant architecture that followed.

*New Brunswick.* The tall tower with a low-pitched roof was the most conspicuous feature of the Italian villa. Pedimented gables, a shallow roof line, and a corner porch were common to the style, as were irregularly grouped round-headed windows. Hood moldings were used in elaborate versions of the style.

*Freehold.* According to Downing, "A villa, however small, in the Italian style may have an elegant and expressive character."

Italian architectural influence gave rise to a second popular form during the Victorian years. One of the most popular styles was the square version of a Renaissance palazzo. It has been given a variety of labels, including Romano-Tuscan, Italianate, and Cube Italian. Its simple lines depended upon window placement and ornament for its richness and, as concern with ornament grew and a decorative vocabulary was developed for the style, it became assimilated as an architectural form and was known as the American Bracketed Villa. Like its more architecturally complex cousin, its popularity, in one version or another, spanned the entire Victorian era.

*Freehold/Allentown.* Originally austere, with low-pitched roof and simple square or rectangular lines, the Italianate house grew more elaborate as fashion demanded, and its plain lines became richly garnished with carved brackets and ornament.

*Cape May City.* Samuel Sloan, a well-known Philadelphia architect, featured the Cube Italian house in his widely used pattern books. He was also the architect of this excellent example of the style.

*Hightstown.* The rich ornament of the bracketed villa often gave it a wedding-cake appearance. The carved brackets were frequently paired, elaborate hood moldings trimmed the windows, and gaudy finials topped the belvedere, lantern, or cupola. Here, double doors marked the entryway, flanked by tall first-floor windows.

*Flemington/Trenton.* It is rare to find a bracketed villa without a prominent veranda. The spacious and inviting introduction led the visitor to an equally light and airy interior. As these houses illustrate, there was room for some variety in the roof line despite the style's fairly rigid limitations.

*Salem*. The best of the Victorian era's several styles was often combined with excellent results, as can be seen in this Cube house that blended Greek and Tuscan with lavish ornament that could only be American.

*Burlington.* Polychrome effects were characteristic of the High Victorian Gothic house. Here, contrasting brickwork is used to create banding and ornament. External woodwork is made to look more solid and details are often heavier than in earlier houses.

*Trenton/Freehold.* The Second Empire, or Mansard, style had its origins in Parisian architecture. Its distinguishing feature was the steep, often curved, line of the double-sloped mansard roof. The size and shape of the windows were also significant. Tall first-floor windows and heavily ornamented arched window heads added surface richness to the symmetrical lines that usually characterized this style.

*Burlington*. The Second Empire style depended heavily on ornament. Here, the practical roof design was garnished with slate tiles in several shapes, which were used to create monochrome patterns and polychrome designs; a coronet of lacy roof cresting and carved ornament on the third-story window arches contribute to the three-dimensionality characteristic of the style.

*Plainfield*. The Second Empire roof rose up from deep cornices supported by brackets. These brackets often formed an ornamental bridge between the roof decoration and the equally interesting trim below.

*Matawan*. The simple silhouette of the Second Empire style was often embellished by a projecting central pavilion topped by a mansard tower rising above the roof line.

*Cape May City.* In an era when more was more, the uncomplicated silhouette of the Mansard house invited ornament and, once embellished, blended with the period's more elaborate styles.

*Belvidere.* The lines of the Mansard style lent themselves easily to the architectural blends popular during the High Victorian era. The elaborate syntax of the style could absorb elements of other forms without the sense of stylistic jumble that was often a part of the architecture of the period.

*Boonton*. Orson Fowler specified that his Octagon style houses be built using "grout" or a "gravel wall." This house is one of the few that looks as if it was built with Fowler's respect for the proper building material.

*Boonton/Cape May.* In its purest form the octagon house was a masonry building. The two octagons shown here, however, were somewhat more conventional frame structures.

*Cape May.* The Stick Style house was characterized by decorative stick-work that gave the appearance of being functional. This "structural" framing was frequently overlaid upon clapboard siding. Spiky roofs were another common feature.

*North Plainfield.* Porch roofs and, often, the main roof were supported by unadorned diagonal braces. Late Stick Style houses were marked by a strong sense of the vertical, which was often intensified by the use of board-and-batten siding.

*Ocean Grove/Island Heights.* Weblike porch ornament and simple but often oversized posts were frequently found on Stick Style houses. Few formal versions of the style remain, but elements appear on many vernacular structures.

*Elberon.* Although much of the stick-work has been removed from this house, the overhanging eaves and plain brackets clearly identify this as a Stick Style house.

The Queen Anne was probably the most exuberant of the High Victorian styles. Although it drew its lines from the medieval English house, it rapidly evolved into a form with so much structural variety that the most significant unifying feature of the thousands of American "Queen Anne" houses was their individuality, expresssed through ragged silhouettes and original combinations of surface forms.

*Bordentown.* Queen Anne designs were included in dozens of pattern books. They were extremely popular throughout New Jersey.

**114** *Island Heights.* Surface variety was an important characteristic of the Queen Anne style. Visual complexities created by the combination of silhouette and projections were often intensified by intricate combinations of shingle work.

*Plainfield.* Seemingly unlimited combinations of exterior materials were used. Shingles were often combined with clapboard, brick, stone, and half-timbering to create a gaudy architectural tapestry.

*Spring Lake.* An irregular silhouette was as important as surface effect. Houses were often topped with conical towers and the complex lines of a multi-gabled roof interrupted by turrets and projecting dormers.

*Detail*. The towers and turrets that were so popular in Queen Anne houses continue to delight the eye.

*Newton.* Porches and balconies contributed to the irregularity of the façade. An encircling veranda, common to the style, provided builders with still another opportunity to install ornament in the form of brackets and balustrades. To insure a parade of visual activity, additional richly carved decorative trim was added.

*Belvidere.* An almost unlimited combination of architectural possibilities were created under the name of Queen Anne. There is an element of surprise in each combination of ornament and structure, as exemplified by the fantastic circle built into this porch.

*Flemington.* Many nineteenth-century houses defy labeling. They reflect the popular choices of an era appropriately described as "the battle of the styles," a time when vernacular blends were built as often as the more easily identified forms.

The second half of the nineteenth century was marked by prosperity and growth in New Jersey cities. Changes in population and land use resulted in the proliferation of the rowhouse, an urban architectural form long familiar to New Jersey.

*Jersey City.* Several rowhouses were frequently built as a single contiguous unit. The prescribed form created stylistic limitations, but resourceful architects and builders managed to include elements of the same stylistic variety that characterized individual houses.

*Detail.* In contrast to the single house, only one rowhouse façade was presented to public view, leaving the architect with a limited opportunity to make a statement. Despite this restriction, rowhouse façades were often bedecked with ornament.

*Newark.* In many cases the trim was inspired by the same forms that were used for individual dwellings. Brackets, fish-scale shingles, and a variety of lintels and hood molds were installed in urban interpretations of French, Italian, Mansard, and Queen Anne styles.

*Jersey City/Hoboken*. Many rowhouses were entered at the parlor floor by a flight of steps. These, too, often provided an opportunity to add ornament.

*Hoboken.* Many of the rowhouses built in New Jersey and New York were constructed from a brown stone quarried in New Jersey. It was so widely used that the term *brownstone* eventually became a popular name for this form of dwelling.

Although most of New Jersey lies above the Mason-Dixon Line, many New Jerseyans had southern sympathies during the Civil War. In 1863 the state legislature went so far as to pass measures seeking an independent peace with the South and rejecting the Emancipation Proclamation. In 1864 a majority of New Jersey voters cast their ballots against Abraham Lincoln. Farmers and manufacturers feared the loss of southern markets, Cape May hotelmen drew many of their patrons from the South, and southern gentlemen traditionally received their education at Princeton. While Jersey "Copperheads and Peace Democrats" worked actively but with little success to stop the war, other Jerseyans went off to fight at Bull Run, Fair Oaks, and Yorktown.

Commercial expansion that had begun before the Civil War gathered momentum in the years immediately following, and the forces that were making villages into cities and converting wilderness crossroads into towns grew stronger. Changes taking place across the United States were mirrored in New Jersey. Rapid industrial growth generated increased wealth and population shifts. Newly built villas, castles, and cottages changed sleepy suburbs and empty fields into urban areas. Quiet main streets became busy downtowns, and rows of cheap, speculative houses were built for the growing labor force.

The houses that people built in New Jersey during these mid-Victorian years were similar to those being built throughout the country. Regional differences were minimized by magazines, pattern books, and builders' guides that offered the same styles to readers all over America. Buildings in Trenton resembled those in Paterson or Camden or, for that matter, Cleveland. The same mansard roofs, Italianate towers, and airy piazzas appeared wherever new houses were built.

In this second architectural phase of the Victorian era, people were less concerned than before with historical authenticity, although architects still drew heavily upon the same early European architecture as a basis for their designs. Calvert Vaux (1824–1895), one of the most widely read pattern book architects, encouraged his readers to take advantage of the variety of structures that the past provided, stating that "all previous experience in architecture is the inherited property of America." He borrowed widely from this legacy in designing the houses in his book, *Villas and Cottages* (1857), which replaced Downing's works as the major architectural influence. Vaux satisfied popular taste by creating combinations of earlier styles and changing their affect by changing their names. Instead of the Italian, Swiss, English, French, or Gothic houses offered by Downing, Vaux called his houses by more general names, such as "a Villa residence with a curved roof," "a suburban house with attics," or "an irregular house without a wing."

Vaux was not alone in presenting more fanciful house forms. Dozens of pattern books were published. Although some became very popular and widely used, others remained regional or little known; most offered similar versions of the same styles. The books usually included information on heating, interiors, ventilation, lectures on the virtues of rural or suburban living, and a fairly standard assortment of cottages, farmhouses, and villas in styles that were modifications of those used earlier. Not only was tremendous variety created by the many blends and combinations, but size and cost were also adapted to meet the needs of various levels of society. "Simple suburban cottages" could be built for fifteen hundred dollars. More elaborate versions cost three thousand dollars, and a variety of villas could be built for sums ranging from fifteen thousand to sixty thousand dollars. The term *picturesque eclecticism* is often used to characterize this period; the phrase well describes the incredible variety of designs (and the occasionally bizarre architectural combinations) found in dwellings built from 1860 until the mid-1880s.

More than a half-dozen distinctive styles were popular. Gothic, Italianate, Second Empire (or Mansard), Stick, Chateauesque, Shingle Queen Anne, and Octagon houses filled in a great deal of New Jersey's previously undeveloped space. The picturesque, flat-roofed tower and asymmetrical façade of the Italianate easily met the requirements of fashion and made Italianate a preferred style at mid-century. Its irregular silhouette also made it the style of transition between the formal lines of early Victorian revivals and the more complex forms that followed.

In addition there were numerous blends, the result of a builder's or owner's fancy. For example, an Italianate house might be pierced with Gothic windows, embellished with Eastlake trim (delicate, linear, engraved ornamental motifs), or given a decorative overlay or ornament that a carpenter could either create himself or, in later years, purchase through catalogs from the local supply yard.

The one characteristic that most of these houses had in common was their picturesque silhouette. Pattern book authors and architects revered the natural and planned houses to harmonize with the landscape. To achieve that end, they, even more than their prewar counterparts, encouraged the use of turrets, towers, balconies, gables, finials, and cresting to develop an asymmetrical appearance and irregular outline. The only exceptions to the picturesque rule were the Mansard and the Octagon, and even these were often modified by turrets or towers to harmonize with popular taste.

The label "High Victorian," often used to describe the period, can also be taken literally. High Victorian houses still rise above their neighbors in many New Jersey towns. Any area where there was growth between 1860 and 1880 usually includes at least one and frequently several houses whose outstanding feature is not just their height but the means by which the impression of height was achieved. Topped with cresting and finials, these houses, with their pointed turrets and gaudy towers, demand one's full, upward-directed attention. They appear to have been designed with architectural glee and share the sense of exuberance and unlimited possibilities that were characteristic of the era during which they were conceived.

In Spring Lake, an imposing seaside resort, this ebullience is reflected in the concentration of houses and hotels that appear to have been built with easy access to heaven in mind. Great conical turrets and towers are made even taller by their trim. Tower ornament, rooftop cresting, and the busy silhouettes create a Victorian version of Camelot. Cape May, too, includes examples of such houses in its panorama of dwellings. Farther north, Hackettstown and Matawan have a few, and these are as splendidly lofty as their more numerous contemporaries along the shore.

## Second Gothic Revival

The Gothic of the high Victorian period is referred to as Second Gothic Revival. Unlike its more somber ancestor, the later form was traditionally built of polychrome materials. The finest examples were often brick accented with banding, with Gothic-inspired brick designs colored differently from the main body of the house. Occasionally, stone and brick were used in combination. Roof lines were often more complex than in the earlier Gothic, and the wooden ornamentation that was added gave the appearance of being structural rather than decorative.

There were many more vernacular interpretations than there were high-style versions. Often the Gothic allusion was found only in an entryway, a steep wall gable, or a pointed dormer window. The Gothic influence was widely felt, however, and in many rural areas where style came late, the wooden variation of the style—Carpenter Gothic— continued to be built until the last years of the century.

In New Jersey there are Second Gothic Revival houses that appear to have come straight from a pattern book. One of the finest is the Grubb house, standing along the Delaware River in Burlington, close by a neighbor that is almost a twin. In these houses the polychrome brickwork, banding, and ornament, exemplary wooden trim, and mandatory Gothic points combine to create nearly perfect examples of the style.

## Second Empire

The Second Empire, or Mansard, house, popular as a dwelling form, has become almost equally popular as a subject for twentieth-century artists and illustrators because of its elegant proportions and pleasant combinations of the curvilinear and the perpendicular. The most striking characteristic of the style is its roof, named for the seventeenth-century architect François Mansard and inspired by the design of the extension of the Louvre that was built during the Second Empire in Paris. The mansard roof is composed of two slopes: the lower, an almost vertical surface with convex or concave sides, and a shallower upper slope that cannot be seen from the ground. This unusual shape provides a full upper story. The dormer window, often elaborately trimmed, is always part of this style. The more elaborate versions have a projecting central pavilion and a tall slender central tower topped by its own mansard, dormer, and pseudo-French ornament. The vertical portion of the mansard roof is often surfaced with octagonal or fish-scale tiles set in a polychrome design. Lacy cresting and structural ornament frequently embellish the roof line.

The best versions of this type of house are richly ornamented. Arched double doors with ornate surrounds and tall, arched first-floor windows, also elaborately trimmed, combine to create a surface richness that enhances the direct lines of the silhouette. Although the form is essentially cubic, towers and projecting pavilions frequently break the smooth façade.

The popularity of the Second Empire style declined within a few years of the French defeat in the Franco-Prussian war in 1871, but before that its popularity was such that many eighteenth- and nineteenth-century houses were "improved" with an unlikely mansard topping. It is not unusual to find a Georgian or Italianate farmhouse that was modernized in this fashion in mid-century, changing its proportions, often for the worse.

## Octagons

One of the most unusual styles to appear in the mid-nineteenth century was the octagon house. Orson Fowler, the phrenologist who developed the style, promised a healthier, better way of life for those who lived in octagon houses. He offered the style to the American public in his book, *A Home for All, or the Gravel Wall and Octagon Mode of Building* (1848). He sought to "improve human homes and especially to bring comfortable dwellings within the reach of the poor classes." The octagon offered increased interior space at little cost. Disliking wood as a building material, Fowler suggested that such houses be built of grout, which he referred to as "the gravel wall," resembling modern-day cement. He explained that the resulting house, with an encircling veranda and cross-ventilation, would provide a healthful environment that was easier to cool and heat and had no dark corners.

Although the octagon house was moderately popular, not many remain. Several do still stand in New Jersey, however, including those in Boonton, Cape May, Hightstown, and Hackettstown. Various building materials, including brick and wood, were used for these houses, but in Boonton one appears to have been constructed with a "gravel wall."

## Stick Style

The Stick Style was so highly regarded that it was chosen by New Jersey to be part of its display at the Philadelphia Centennial Exposition in 1876. Unlike Fowler's octagons, Stick Style houses were designed to utilize the appearance of wood, believed by the style's advocates to be a uniquely American building material. Some historians consider it an interpretive, simplified form of the Second Gothic Revival, while others connect it to the Swiss Chalet. Despite these European connections it is generally thought of as a purely American architectural phenomenon. The Stick Style's structural "truthfulness" made it compatible with mid-Victorian ideals. "Truthfulness," curiously, was manifested in the use of exterior trim to simulate the supporting inner structure. Unembellished diagonal stick-work and intersecting boards were placed over the siding, which was usually clapboard. "Truth" continued in equally unembellished diagonal brackets that were used to support roofs and porches.

The classic Stick Style house was picturesquely designed, using a variety of gables, porches, dormers, and balconies to create an irregular silhouette. It was developed with a strong sense of the vertical. Often, exterior structural embellishments include rows of perpendicular trim that surround porches and face the surfaces of gables to accentuate the style's verticality.

The 1877 Emlen Physick house in Cape May is a nationally known example of Stick Style that is attributed to Frank Furness (1839–1912). Steep, spiky roofs top a clapboard exterior that is neatly enclosed by exterior pseudo-framing. Porches and wings contribute to the silhouette, and curved porch brackets lighten the grand scale.

Classic Stick houses are not common in New Jersey. In vernacular houses, stick detailing may be restricted to brackets and upper gables, or a small balcony. Sometimes the only Stick detail is found on a simple front porch.

## Queen Anne

The Queen Anne house was the embodiment of the high Victorian architectural ideal. A version of the style was first seen in this country at the Philadelphia Centennial Exposition, when the British government erected two such dwellings to house its staff. The style was received with great enthusiasm by American architects and builders and was cited by one publication for "its wonderful adaptability to this country." Indeed, Queen Anne houses were built across America during the succeeding decades.

Queen Anne houses were, and are, the ultimate in picturesque—riotous collations of architectural elements, usually including at least one tower, several projecting gables, verandas, dormers, recessed porches, projecting bays, and pseudo-half-timber trim creating the complex façade essential to the style. Structural intricacy continues in the choice and combination of materials. It is rare to find a house of this genre that has fewer than three different exterior surfaces. Often, several different styles of shingling were combined with stone, brickwork, and wooden siding. Three-dimensional terra cotta and plaster garlands, carved and turned ornament, and half-timbering were among the materials used. Even the small vernacular versions of the Queen Anne that fill New Jersey were built with the same structural exuberance of the grander versions, using a variety of materials and ornament.

Queen Anne houses stand wherever there was late nineteenth-century construction. Often entire neighborhoods form an optical jumble of porches, gables, and turrets. Because of its complexity, the Queen Anne house provided builders and owners the greatest opportunities to satisfy their creative impulses. The nature of the style spawned a form of eclecticism that left a legacy as varied as it is complex. New Jersey Queen Annes offer a structural range that dazzles the observer. The variety to be found in porch trim alone is nearly boundless.

## City Cousins

Houses that were built in the cities at this time were quite different from those in suburbs and rural areas. Densely populated communities like Trenton, Newark, Jersey City, Hoboken, and Elizabeth could no longer accommodate the single house surrounded by land and trees. Instead, central urban residential areas were largely filled with rows of contiguous houses fronting upon the street, frequently without so much as a patch of lawn at the front door.

The American rowhouse was not a new phenomenon. Houses in Trenton's Mill Hill date back to the first half of the nineteenth century. Many of Burlington's are even older. Post–Civil War growth in the cities was so great, however, that the houses built then became a significant factor in reshaping both the appearance of cities and the way people lived.

Many materials were used to build rowhouses. Brick was popular. Frame was used occasionally. It was brownstone, however, that made the greatest impact upon the urban landscape and became almost a synonym for the city rowhouse. The stone that was used was itself a New Jersey phenomenon. Called Belleville stone, it was quarried in several areas in the northeastern part of the state.

In some ways the rowhouses stylistically resembled their suburban cousins, but the nature of their structure imposed limitations. Exterior ornament was limited to the front of the house. Common sidewalls and a rear façade not seen by the public left the architect with only one side on which to develop a style and place ornament.

At first glance, many of these houses appear almost uniform. Important front steps lead to a parlor floor with two tall windows and high ceilings. There are usually two more floors, with smaller windows. Rowhouses were often built as a single unit, and their façades formed one continuous surface broken only by windows, doors, steps, and ornament.

Despite these design limitations, builders found ways to include a variety of style and ornament. Some of the most creative Victorian ornament and clearest expressions of popular styles can be found carved in heavy stone rowhouses. These houses are described in the *Old-House Journal* as maintaining "the essence of various styles. . . . Doorways with fanlights and sidelights in Federal, arched windows and heavy brackets of Italianate; . . . Mansard roof with countless dormer variations;

dentilled corners with classic column and architrave on Greek revival doorways; dazzling variety of gable, bays, textures and horizontal banding on Queen Anne." But this was only the beginning. A variety of sculptural ornament was created to embellish these structures further. Garlands, cherubs, faces, classically inspired forms, and ornate ironwork were set into walls, inlaid into door and window moldings, added to front steps, and occasionally included as part of the frieze under the roof cornice. These buildings have as part of their exterior ornament elaborate carvings and sculptural additions that transform them from simple dwellings into complex works of art.

In Newark, Jersey City, Hoboken, and other cities of the era, there are block after block of brownstones. Despite their apparent homogeneity these houses can be distinguished from each other by their ornament. Differences in doorways, window shapes, and ornament at the roof line add to each house's special quality.

Brick city houses, too, offer forms of urban splendor. Jersey City has row upon row of brick houses, including one street where the houses are joined by the continuous lacy ironwork of balconylike porches and stair rails. Rows of brick townhouses also enclose a Jersey City square that is considered by some to have an almost Georgian quality. In Hoboken, Newark, and Jersey City, as well as Trenton, Paterson, and many other of the state's urban areas, are blocks of contiguous houses that appear to have been individually designed and built. These include chateaus, Dutch replicas, Romanesques, and other more elegant and weighty styles in a variety of imposing masonry materials.

Bergen Hill in Jersey City and sections of Hoboken, Trenton, Newark, and the state's many other late-nineteenth-century cities also include neighborhoods with impressive houses that were never meant to be mansions but clearly sought to provide an elegant setting for those who built and lived in them. They are especially meaningful if we remember that they represent great care and an ability to create beauty in a way that is probably no longer possible. No more craftsmen will carve a garland, a nymph, or a Viking face over the doorway of a middle-class house. Nor will many people attempt to link their houses, and thus their lives, to imperial splendor by emulating the windows and doorways created for emperors and kings.

# Turn-of-the-Century Changes

*Pennington.* A combination of shingle and stone was frequently used. This blend of materials is often seen in houses whose silhouettes reflect the architectural eccentricity of the Queen Anne house rather than the less complicated mass peculiar to the Shingle Style.

The Victorian penchant for ornament peaked with the Queen Anne style. As the twentieth century approached, architecture became more restrained. Elements of the Queen Anne and other High Victorian styles remained, but they were expressed in a more conservative and less attractive mode. Towers were shorter; trim —often machine-made— was coarser, heavier, and less frequently used. The Shingle Style, which had enjoyed modest popularity for some years, became the style of transition. It embraced other forms but developed a definite character of its own. In the last years of its popularity, the style was used in both innovative and traditional modes, largely because of the design flexibility of the wooden shingle itself. It evolved into a form of the Colonial Revival, a style that dominated the early decades of this century; at the same time more innovative architects, including Frank Lloyd Wright, were also designing shingle houses using the simpler lines that began with the Prairie Style.

*Rumson*. At the end of the nineteenth century commuter and resort communities in New Jersey attracted affluent populations. Their houses, often of shingle, were grandiose and characterized by a sense of great mass.

*Elberon*. Shingle was popular for the great "cottages" that once dotted the New Jersey shore. They were often designed by the most important architects of the time, such as Charles Follen McKim, who created this Colonial-inspired dwelling for Moses Taylor.

*Freehold.* Shingle was also widely used for more modest dwellings. These took many forms, ranging from workmen's rowhouses to smaller versions of the high-style house to simple gambrel structures like this one.

*Bordentown*. The adaptability of the Shingle Style allowed it to be used in the transitional structures that evolved into the more formal Colonial Revival.

*Plainfield.* Although masonry was the preferred material for the round-arched Romanesque Revival house, the adaptable shingle lent itself nicely to vernacular versions of the style. In this example, credit must be given to more than one architectural form, but the strongest statement is clearly made by the Romanesque arch, a motif repeated here in ornament as well as structure.

*Trenton*. The heavy lines of Richardsonian Romanesque, a masonry version of the round-arched style, were usually restricted to commercial and institutional structures. They can occasionally be found in residential versions. The massive rock-faced arch is the distinguishing feature of this style.

As the century turned, American homebuilders again looked to the past. Another era of revivals began, and versions of English cottages, Tudor manors, Colonial dwellings, and a smattering of chateaus and minor palaces filled once empty lots.

*Montclair*. There was a version of the English house for almost everyone. Size ranged from tiny cottages to dwellings on so grand a scale that they might have sheltered ghosts of English royalty.

*Princeton.* The half-timbered house was widely built in the affluent commuter villages. The style had a wide public, including Woodrow Wilson, who lived in this house for several years.

*West Long Branch.* The Colonial styles, which gradually returned to favor during the last decades of the nineteenth century, were probably the most popular of the revival forms. They remained so for many years, occurring in elaborate, architect-designed houses as well as in vernacular versions. In this house, Stanford White combined the Victorian sense of ornament with the more restrained symmetry and lines of the Georgian style.

*Plainfield.* Revival fervor often went to extremes of fidelity, as in this line-for-line copy of the well-known Longfellow house in Cambridge. It has lost its balustrade, but in every other respect duplicates the original Georgian dwelling built in 1759.

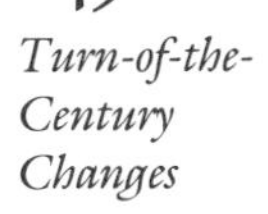

*Montclair*. The Colonial Revival included Georgian and Federal elements. Often a ghost of Victorian taste remained within the orderly Palladian lines of these houses.

*Princeton*. The Dutch Colonial, an early New Jersey house form, was much used throughout the nation. Its popularity cut across social and economic lines, and the gambrel roof soon appeared on thousands of dwellings, both modest and grand.

While most of the nation seemed content with versions of the older styles, there were those who sought new forms for their dwellings. Much of the more radical architectural activity took place in the Midwest, but New Jersey was not without influence in shaping the newer form of American dwelling.

*Morris Plains.* Gustav Stickley led a national movement to simplify style in housing and furnishings. His philosophy was expressed clearly in the unpretentious lines of his own home, Craftsman Farms. Log and native stone, used simply, mirror Stickley's concern with the direct use of materials.

*Cape May/Princeton.* Bungalows were frequently featured in the pages of Stickley's *Craftsman.* They were small, often one story, with porch and gable end facing the street. Their popularity is reflected in the rows and rows of bungalows that form entire neighborhoods throughout the nation.

Queen Victoria died in 1901. Although her death marked the official closing of an era characterized by dramatic change, the Victorian way of life was by no means dead. In the United States, ebullient optimism, self-satisfaction, and a sense of never-ending prosperity and progress persisted until change was forced upon the nation by World War I. Technological developments, spawned by the nation's continuing growth, significantly influenced the nature of the house. By the end of the nineteenth century, electricity and indoor plumbing were providing previously unheard of comforts and shaping interior house design.

New Jersey cities continued to expand. Growing industrial facilities drew thousands of factory laborers and their families. The dramatically increased need for manpower combined with difficult conditions in Europe to draw Italians, Russians, Poles, Hungarians, and Swedes to "the land of plenty." The state government tried to attract the immigrants to New Jersey by distributing tracts and broadsides praising its soil and climate. One such document went so far as to compare the climate with that of the Mediterranean.

Over half a million immigrants settled in the state, finding work in its thriving clay pits, refineries, mines, and mills. By 1901 New Jersey ranked fifth nationally in total number of immigrants. Many of these new arrivals settled in the cities, where the sudden population increase encouraged speculative building and an increased number of rental units. Conditions were difficult and decent shelter was rare. Various philanthropic groups established some new communities in rural areas in an effort to improve conditions for the immigrants. Farm-factory towns such as Woodbine, Norma, Rosenhaub, and Alliance were cleared from the South Jersey wilderness, and homes and factories were built. In the new towns people were able to live simply, grow their own food, and earn their living.

Quite different living conditions existed in other parts of the state for a small but influential segment of the population. During the last decades of the century millionaires hired such famous architects as Charles Follen McKim (1847–1909), Stanford White (1853–1906), the firm of McKim, Mead and White, Henry Hudson Holly, and Carrère and Hastings to design not-so-simple frame "cottages" and elegant Beaux-Arts manor houses in Long Branch, Montclair, Elberon, Short Hills, Rumson, Morristown and other prosperous commuting and resort towns. Havens for the affluent, in the manner of Tuxedo Park and Newport, grew up between Deal and Sandy Hook. Grandly proportioned houses with large, airy porches and dozens of windows faced the southeasterly currents that blew along the ocean bluff.

Near the end of the nineteenth century, Long Branch ranked as one of the three great watering places in America, together with Saratoga and Newport. At one time it claimed the largest hotel in the United States, which stood along the shore among other equally imposing structures. Long Branch remained a summer retreat for the rich and powerful through the early years of the twentieth century. Today almost all traces of this era are gone. Most of the structures that rose above the dune grasses and sandy soil have disappeared, together with the way of life that they sheltered. Some have been destroyed, others left to run down, while many have fallen victim to the eroding currents that constantly reshape the shore.

The salubrious effects of the New Jersey shore were so highly regarded that when President Garfield was wounded by an assassin he was brought to the seaside to convalesce. The railroad obligingly laid track overnight in order to bring the President directly to Franklyn cottage in Elberon. Unfortunately even the New Jersey seaside could not heal the President's wounds; and two weeks later, he died.

Franklyn cottage, like those of equal scale built during the last decades of the nineteenth century, was an exemplary version of the simpler houses built throughout the country. It could be distinguished from its poorer relations by scale and attention to detail —which was often fine and used in abundance.

## The Shingle Style

Although for a time many of the "Shingle" houses built in New Jersey were essentially Queen Anne houses within a shingle exterior, the classic Shingle house is quite the opposite of the visually active Queen Anne. Instead of the picturesque, the ideal Shingle house was designed to create a sense of great mass, partly because of the simplified silhouette and partly through the use of a single dark material for the exterior. Siding and roof were usually both of shingle and presented an uninterrupted shape, which often included shingle-encased porch pillars as well. Occasionally the first story and the pillars were built of rubble or heavy stone, but this only added to the satisfyingly ponderous effect.

A strong sense of the horizontal was also characteristic of the Shingle Style. This effect was the result of the parallel sets of horizontal lines created where one row of shingles met the next, by bands of wooden trim, painted in a contrasting color, that often encircled the house, and by horizontally oriented window groupings.

Examples of almost every version of the Shingle house can be seen along the New Jersey shore. Perhaps the greatest concentration of these houses stands in Bay Head, an oceanside village consisting almost entirely of Shingle Style homes. Bay Head dwellings are generally more modest than the larger, more ornate cottages in nearby communities, but they include a number of rather grand and quite typical summer houses of the period as well as many smaller versions.

Most of the great Shingle houses, however, were built farther north, in Elberon, Long Branch, Rumson, and Sea Bright, areas with easier access to the cities. Stanford White, Bruce Price, and Charles McKim were among the noted architects whose firms designed these houses. Even the U.S. Army was not exempt from the influence of fashion. Several Shingle houses were designed as officers' summer quarters at Fort Hancock and were grand enough to have been attributed at one time to Stanford White.

Every New Jersey town that predates 1910 has at least one, and probably several, Shingle houses. Important versions stand in Montclair, the Oranges, and similar affluent commuter towns of the period. Often they, like the even grander homes of the very rich, were designed by famous architects such as Henry Hudson Holly, Alexander F. Oakey, Joy Wheeler Dow, and the firms of McKim, Mead and White or Lamb and Rich. But the style was in no way restricted to important buildings. The Shingle mode was easily used in all manner of vernacular houses, and a "real" Shingle house can include many stylistic elements and forms. Some have gambrel roofs, others Romanesque arches, while still others boast Palladian windows and other Georgian features.

## Romanesque

Elements of the Romanesque, or round-arched, style can be found in houses that span the Victorian era. The original Romanesque Revival took place in mid-century but was largely restricted to churches and public buildings. Like almost every other style, however, in some fashion it was assimilated into popular taste, and the round arch began to appear in houses. It easily became a part of the Shingle Style, and round-arched porches, supports, and gable windows were popular for a time. It reached its highest point, however, in Richardsonian Romanesque, a masonry style that was in fashion during the 1870s and 1880s.

Henry Hobson Richardson (1838–1886) is still remembered for his Stick and Shingle designs as well as for his later Romanesque work. In 1872 the Beaux-Arts-trained architect designed Trinity Church in Copley Square in Boston. Here he adapted the Romanesque style by using rock-faced masonry and accenting the arches and other details by facing them with stone different from that used in walls. This particular use of the stone surface created an effect that was radically different from earlier Romanesque because of its great visual weight. Richardsonian Romanesque was widely used throughout the country for churches and commercial structures. In New Jersey it can be seen occasionally in the cities, where the more costly masonry houses were built. Few single-family dwellings were ever completely executed in this massive and costly style, but some townhouses were built with the dramatic archways that seemed to promise deep, dark spaces beyond.

Romanesque details were often used in Shingle houses, since their proportions fit easily into the scale of the Shingle Style and Romanesque lines made a positive contribution to the sought-after sense of mass.

## Transition

Toward the end of the nineteenth century, the many versions of the Shingle house began to fall from favor, and styles began to reflect the two major directions in which American architecture was heading. Styles were no longer acceptable to conservative and radical alike; a conflict between progressives and traditionalists was forming. Each faction became associated with a distinct approach to form. The radicals chose to extrapolate and extend the simplified lines and strong horizontal movements that had begun in the Shingle silhouette. The traditionalists, who were in the majority, preferred familiar forms and began another period of revivals, this time academically correct versions of historic styles.

The appearance of many late Shingle houses neatly reflected more conservative tastes. The many manifestations of the style gradually disappeared, and the Shingle became the form of transition between the picturesque and the more restrained Georgian (or Colonial) Revival, a style that continues to be a favorite. Shingle houses began to have increasing amounts of colonial detail, where previously such detail had been used to only a minor degree. Palladian windows, classical columns, broken pediments, and all the other features that were characteristic of Georgian houses reappeared and were soon accepted by all but the radicals.

## New Ideas

For the first time there was open conflict among architectural leaders. *American Architect and Building News* (which had begun publishing in 1876) spoke out against originality, and instead encouraged the plethora of revival styles that were beginning to influence all forms of building. While the conservative majority marched backward in architectural time, others moved toward the belief that the exterior design of the house should be an original, creative statement and that the interior layout should be adapted to meet the needs of those who lived within. Using and going beyond the forms of the Shingle Style, progressive architects created simpler, more functional houses that ultimately evolved into more clearly contemporary styles. This movement was strongest in the Midwest, and the clean lines and strong horizontal movements characteristic of much midwestern architecture came to be identified as the Prairie School.

*Gustav Stickley.* In New Jersey, Gustav Stickley (1858–1942), originally from Wisconsin, was preaching the virtues of the nontraditional house. In his magazine *The Craftsman,* which first appeared in 1901, Stickley's individualistic approach and his concern with the naturalness of form reflected public reaction to the anonymity of style fostered by the use of machines and to new demands placed upon people by industrial society. Stickley stressed the value of handcraftsmanship, functional architectural design, and "the wholesome lesson of simplicity," while discouraging "large houses with many rooms" and styles that evoked the past.

"The influence of the home," according to Stickley, "is of the first importance in shaping character." To this end he discouraged complex floor plans and ornate house design, stating that the need for luxury would bring the nation to "the brink of degeneration." Instead, he offered plans that "would simplify the work of home life and add to its wholesome joy." In an article in *The Craftsman,* Samuel Howe reported the following dialogue: "*Visitor:* 'Have you no ornament, carving or draperies in your house, Mr. Stickley?' *Stickley:* 'No draperies thank you, and as for ornament, have we not our friends?' "

*The Craftsman* and *Craftsman Homes* were published from Stickley's own home, Craftsman Farms, in Morris Plains. The house, which is still standing, embodied his concern with the direct expression of materials. Its simple outline and the use of logs and stones for the exterior surfaces were a harmonious statement of the Craftsman ideal, in direct contrast to the mannered Colonial Revival.

Stickley made his house designs easily available to the public. A notice in the 1909 edition of *Craftsman Homes* stated, "To anyone sending us $3.00 for a year's subscription to THE CRAFTSMAN we will send blue prints . . . plans . . . , elevations from which . . . houses can be built." The ready accessibility of inexpensive plans for economical houses that could be run without servants resulted in the proliferation of *Craftsman*-inspired structures. The houses, designed with economy and functional needs in mind, often cost as little as eighteen hundred dollars to build.

*Craftsman*-inspired houses abound in most New Jersey towns and cities, but they are simply constructed, unadorned structures that often are passed without notice. Although they seem to lack grace and concern for design, these houses are as significant for what they are not as for what they are. They are not plain because nobody cared, but because somebody thought it was important to be plain.

These houses marked the beginning of a new middle-class way of life that fell between the economic extremes the industrial nation was capable of producing. Their lack of adornment and their practical interiors also formed a bridge between the Victorian confections that preceded them and the more organic house design that became the basis of a later architectural vocabulary. Most important, though, these houses represented homes that worked; they were built to satisfy an aesthetic and to meet specific human needs "just as simply as possible."

*Bungalows.* The bungalow, popularized in Stickley's *Craftsman*, continued to be widely built even after World War I. Although the bungalow's heyday was during the first two decades of the twentieth century, the Bungalowcraft Company, for example, was offering books of "the newest homes" for one dollar, as late as 1928. These houses were inexpensive to build and plans were easily obtained through the popular magazines. "California Bungalow Books," "Kozy Home Bungalows," and "Artistic Bungalows" were among those that were advertised in *House Beautiful* and the *Ladies Home Journal*.

Although the widest use of the bungalow style was in California, a trip through any area of New Jersey built before the Depression reveals that it met the needs of a large segment of the public. Many of the early lake communities in the northwestern part of the state consist largely of bungalows. The "classical" bungalow, which had its origins in India, was only a single floor, but many of those in New Jersey include a half-story above the first.

Despite the economical design of their homes, bungalow owners sought the same variety of style as those who built more complex, expensive dwellings. Bungalows were built using almost as many different styles as the larger, grander houses of the period; English, Spanish, Colonial, Swiss Chalet, and Prairie style were but a few.

*Joy Wheeler Dow.* The work of Joy Wheeler Dow has also been grouped with that of the progressives. The houses he built fall somewhere between the faithful revivals of the academicians and the more daring work of the progressive realists. From the vantage point of the late twentieth century his early-century shingle houses and English cottages appear conservative, but he was considered eclectic and somewhat radical because he stressed adaptations of traditional forms rather than replicas.

Wheeler received national recognition for his writings on architecture as well as for his houses. In his influential book, *American Renaissance,* and in his articles that appeared in collections and publications, he often used as examples houses in popular styles that he had designed in New Jersey.

Houses designed by Wheeler can be found in Summit, Short Hills, and elsewhere in the state. On the hill above Wyoming Avenue in Millburn are several small Wheeler-designed houses in a variety of styles. They are remarkable for their handcrafted detail, an unusual characteristic in a machine-dominated age.

## Popular Conservatism

A few houses were built in New Jersey by the more progressive architects of the Chicago school, but most of those of the late nineteenth and early twentieth century were in the more conservative revival styles and simpler late versions of Victorian styles. Most of these fell between their more elaborate Victorian ancestors and the less complicated structures that were to come. The increasing desire for historically accurate, more decorous architecture resulted in houses that maintained some characteristics of the picturesque eclecticism of the earlier houses but became self-conscious. In the process, much was lost. Historically correct trim put a damper on decorative exuberance. The desire for a more regular silhouette led to houses that were almost cowardly in scale. Towers rose up timidly from squat silhouettes. Unfortunately, the vernacular house, which represented the great majority of late-nineteenth-century buildings, became a structure without imagination and without the daring combinations that had made the earlier houses so glamorous and exciting to contemplate. Cube Italian houses became bracketless boxes; Queen Anne was frequently expressed by a projecting dormer on an otherwise unembellished structure; towers and turrets became stubby; and exterior materials became more uniform and less interesting.

Late Victorian houses were built well into the twentieth century. They fill many of New Jersey's older towns. They rarely catch the eye, but if they do, it is seldom because they are attractive, but rather because they seem such a contrast to the houses that preceded them. Still, they are a reminder of a time, and of people who chose such houses for themselves because they represented current taste and fashion, and because they, like their more interesting predecessors, reflected changes in architectural taste.

The two most popular revival forms were the English half-timbered house (popularly called stockbroker Tudor) and the dozens of versions of the early American house that were collectively known as Colonial Revival.

English half-timbered houses quickly became the architecture of choice for stockbrokers, bankers, manufacturers, and even Woodrow Wilson, who chose this style for his Princeton home. It was so popular that before the last nail was driven, he found a near duplicate rising almost opposite his own.

In towns like Montclair, Plainfield, and Westfield, entire neighborhoods still resemble the outskirts of an English village. Heavy dark beams form patterns and shadows on a background of cream-colored masonry walls. Great trees and rich collections of shrubbery—so essential to this style—almost mask many of these houses from the public eye, but most were executed on such a grand scale that their romantic exteriors can be divined within their woody settings.

At the same time that the well-to-do were filling their neighborhoods with half-timbered manor houses, more modest versions were being built in less affluent areas. These houses were often taken from pattern books, which continued to be the major source of vernacular houses. Magazines, too, offered an assortment of plans that could be obtained for a small fee. The magazines usually offered plans in the more conventional popular revival styles, but even the work of Frank Lloyd Wright, who was then becoming a well-known force in American architecture, was available. (In the February 1901 *Ladies Home Journal*, "A Home in a Prairie Town" was included as part of the *Journal's* "New Series of Model Suburban Houses which Can be Built at Moderate Cost.") More in keeping with its usual offerings, the *Journal* presented in March 1901 a half-timbered structure, including six bedrooms and a sewing room, that could be built for sixty-five hundred dollars.

While some neighborhoods were developing in an English mode, others were reaching back to America's past for their house designs. Joy Wheeler Dow referred to "everyone's Patriotism" as a force that should assist in developing the Colonial Revival. Whether it was patriotism or fashion that did the trick, there is no doubt of the widespread public acceptance of the Colonial Revival. Houses that were often nearly duplicates of those built 150 years earlier appeared everywhere.

The Colonial Revival had begun to gather momentum in the mid-1880s; Charles McKim had built some of the earliest "imitation colonials" in Montrose in the 1870s. The style did not sweep the country, however, until the turn of the century. Magazine articles in popular and professional journals encouraged an architectural nostalgia that increased in succeeding decades. *Harper's Magazine* published romantic accounts of the trials and hardships of the colonists. These articles gave the past a new glamor and expressed a popular desire for a return to "smaller, simpler and more natural things." The Centennial in 1876 generated popular interest in things colonial. *American Architecture* suggested that architects make notes on colonial buildings because of their superior style and "good breeding."

The New Jersey Dutch farmhouse was one of the "colonial" forms that received a great deal of attention at this time. It was cited by J. Cleveland Cady in a talk given in 1877 to the New York chapter of the Association of American Architects. He referred to the "Dutch" house as "simple" and "expressive, . . . seeming to have grown out of the hillside. . . the timbered and ceiled ceiling . . . far prettier in color and light and shade than any expanse of plaster could be." Cady also spoke of the "broad horizontal lines," which in fact became important in another architectural context within a few years.

Although the earliest Colonial Revivals were the shingle versions of the style, it was not long before brick, clapboard, stone, and stucco were used to build all manner of early-style houses. Accuracy of detail and careful crafting often made it difficult to distinguish between bona fide early houses and twentieth-century copies. The same Palladian windows, classical ornament, and roof lines were incorporated into the newer versions. Sometimes the only visible difference was that the newer houses were grander than their prototypes. The instinct for blending was not quite dead, however, and there were a fair number of Colonial Revivals that mixed Federal, Greek Revival, and Georgian elements. Thousands of these houses exist in New Jersey. Like the English half-timbered house, they were widely built in the affluent commuter towns as well as in less populous areas.

The Colonial Revival was also very popular as a vernacular form. There is no danger of mistaking the popular version of the Colonial Revival house for the original. Unlike its more expensive cousins, it was not architecturally interesting and was, instead, often an economical solution to building a house. It was structurally simple, with a standard interior plan, and rarely included sufficient detail to make it noteworthy.

The "colonial"—which continues to be one of the most popular styles—has never fallen from favor in New Jersey, or elsewhere in the country. It not only continues to be built for individuals but springs up by the hundreds in major subdivisions. "Colonial" details even appear in such modern structural crossbreeds as the split-level and the raised ranch, two forms that house much of twentieth-century New Jersey.

# After the War

During the past fifty years examples of significant domestic architecture have been built in this state, including a few in the vanguard of architectural fashion. Some, such as the communities of Radburn, Roosevelt, and Twin Rivers, represent attempts to initiate social change as much as architectural growth. Others reflect the continuing search for more daring and creative methods of designing houses.

*Radburn.* Radburn was the first planned garden suburb designed to shield its residents from the impact of the automobile. Houses face a common landscaped expanse with walkways meandering through a tunnel that leads beneath the roadway to the next common area.

*Roosevelt.* Although Roosevelt was conceived as a social experiment to enrich the lives of urban workers, the Bauhaus-inspired houses have lasted far longer than the original concept.

*Millstone.* Frank Lloyd Wright favored horizontal movements that would create a harmonious connection between the houses he designed and their surroundings. Here, great expanses of glass were used to visually integrate the interior with the surrounding countryside.

*Princeton.* In 1947 the Museum of Modern Art commissioned Marcel Breuer to design a house in the contemporary idiom that would meet the needs of a middle-class American family. This mirror-image of that innovative structure displays the clean lines and sweeping movements that were considered radical at the time and have since become part of popular concepts of American architectural style.

*Princeton*. In this innovative addition to a traditional house, Michael Graves, one of the leading post-modernist architects, expresses the continuing concern with new forms and the search for new ways of using older forms that has always characterized American domestic architecture.

*Twin Rivers.* The enormous housing needs of late twentieth century also require new solutions. Unlike earlier planned communities, this newest form offers its inhabitants an instant city.

World War I caused significant changes in New Jersey. Munitions works, oil refineries, textile factories, and many other industries flourished. Planned communities such as Allwood, in Passaic, were built to house the increased number of workers. Many war-related products were made in Kearney, Camden, Newark, Plainfield, Linden, and dozens of other New Jersey cities. Boom towns and company towns, often jerry-built, sprang up from nothing.

Many American soldiers passed through New Jersey on their way "over there," using Hoboken as a major port of embarkation. In order to accommodate them, the area around Wrightstown, a village of fewer than fifty houses, was rapidly transformed into a base with over sixteen hundred buildings housing seventy thousand troops, as well as horses and machinery; it was named Fort Dix. Before the war was over there were fifteen more military bases in the state.

When the war ended, change continued at an even faster pace. The state's long coastline became a haven for bootleggers, and the corridor state opened its traffic lanes to the rum runners.

The opening of the Delaware River Bridge in 1926, followed by the Holland Tunnel in 1927, and later, the Lincoln Tunnel, and the George Washington Bridge, made it easy to move all kinds of goods as well as increasing numbers of people in and out of the state.

By this time the automobile had become part of life in America. It not only was a common mode of travel but also generated countless social and material changes. The auto freed people from their dependence on the railroad and the need to live in cities close to their jobs. Although cars were costly at first, prices were steadily reduced by manufacturing efficiency. By 1926 it cost only $260 to own a Model T. By 1930 there were over 20 million cars in use. The car changed people's ideas of where they could live. With the advent of the popularly priced car in the mid-1920s, it was possible to live or travel anywhere there was a road. Once remote areas became suitable locations for home building. And, frequently, urban amenities, such as shops, were not far behind.

## Planned Communities

As America took to the roads, the concept of the landscaped suburb that had had its beginnings in Llewellyn Park became a reality throughout the nation. As block after block of houses were built in outlying areas, creating the beginnings of suburban sprawl, architects became increasingly concerned about the character of communities as entities rather than as collections of independent structures. Many of the resulting ideas were gleaned from the work of an Englishman named Ebenezer Howard. His book, *Garden Cities of Tomorrow,* described small, beautifully landscaped, self-contained, and self-supporting cities.

Widespread interest in the planned suburb was reflected in the *House Beautiful* Annual Building Issue of 1929. Oakcroft, a group of houses built around a single open space in Ridgewood, was cited for its use of the common area as part of the original plan. Radburn, in Fair Lawn, designed and developed by Clarence Stein and Henry Wright, soon followed.

Radburn was one of the earliest planned communities in America. It was probably the first town to be designed to protect its residents from being dominated by the demands of the automobile. Although the design permitted easy access by car, it did not allow the automobile to intrude or to control living patterns. This carefully landscaped village, begun in 1928, was planned with pedestrian walkways and bicycle paths that passed beneath the roadways, avoiding contact with any cars. The creation of the superblock, with cluster housing at its periphery, permitted trees and greensward unbroken by roadways. The houses, which included single-family as well as multiple dwellings, had attractive façades at both front and rear, since the common parkland behind the houses was considered as aesthetically important as the entryways.

Radburn, which is now surrounded by Fair Lawn, was planned to be self-sufficient. It was designed to accommodate a large enough population to support its own schools, commercial areas, and industry but small enough to retain a sense of community. Timing was unfortunate, however, for the Depression caused building to stop before Radburn was even half-finished. Enough of the proposed community was built, however, for it to become a modest version of its original concept. Radburn today has changed little, and the excellence of the concept is still easy to see. Footpaths and roadways remain separate. Lovely green areas are easily accessible, and the design clearly benefits the quality of daily life.

## Between the Wars

Before the Depression all but put a stop to house building in New Jersey, there was a period of great expansion. The combined effects of postwar prosperity, increased use of the car, and the accompanying growth of highways resulted in the expansion of existing commuter suburbs and the filling in of a good deal of the state's open spaces. Despite the popular desire for up-to-date interiors—modern amenities like indoor plumbing and electricity were becoming a reality for an increasing number of people—most of the public continued to prefer architectural styles whose origins were in the past. An article in *House Beautiful* on the "Antecedents of the American House" describes the "conveniences as essentially a product of the times" but the exterior as "an inheritance from the distant past." It was a time for a return to more romantic houses and cozy English cottages; Tudor revivals and the various permutations and combinations of "colonial" architecture appeared everywhere. The same styles in varying forms were used by those who were still building manor houses and those who built more modest dwellings.

The diverse architectural preferences of the early twentieth century are apparent throughout New Jersey. Although the range is somewhat greater in affluent areas, modest homes, too, reflect public desire for stylistic variety. This can be seen in popular pattern books for smaller houses that seek to convey a sense of grandeur. In one book a five-room house is praised: "This little home proves that size is not necessary for distinction." This was not really the case, however, and the state is filled with small-scale, uninspired but comfortable versions of the significant styles. In the *New York Times,* Paul Goldberger recently noted that "none . . . are seriously innovative, but all are decent, with functional, matter of fact floor plans, easy room arrangements and plenty of light and air. That is not only more than the historical architecture that inspired these houses could often provide; it is also more than many architects of custom-designed houses in the 1920s could provide. It is architecture as a romantic image."

After the stock market crashed, the new housing erected in the state was quite different. Communities of crude shacks, often made of tin and other scrap material, were built in the Jersey Meadows, a vast, swampy no-man's land not far from Newark. These flimsy, jerry-built "Hoovervilles" were the only shelter for many victims of the great financial disaster.

## Government Builders

Fortunately, all the construction by-products of the Depression were not so disastrous. A spate of federally funded projects designed to provide employment resulted in the improvement of public facilities and historically significant houses. The Works Projects Administration (WPA) hired men and women for enterprises that ranged from the construction of a Greek amphitheater to the restoration of Grover Cleveland's birthplace in Caldwell.

One of the most notable efforts to improve local living standards during the Depression was the creation of the community of Jersey Homesteads, now known as Roosevelt. The small village, just outside Hightstown, was developed in the early 1930s by the federal government as a social experiment: it was an attempt to establish a cooperative, self-supporting community that would remove its residents from many of the hardships of urban life. Original plans included self-contained industrial facilities and sufficient land for each dwelling to permit residents to grow their own produce. Louis Kahn, who later became a major figure in American architecture, assisted Alfred Kastner in designing the village of small, Bauhaus-style residences, a factory, and, later, a school. At the time, the boxlike cinderblock-and-concrete houses were quite radical in concept. There was little adornment to break the stark lines, but they were economical, practical, and used glass dramatically in the living room. Although decades of prosperity have permitted additions and alterations, the overall physical character of Roosevelt remains much as it did during its early years.

Despite its success as a place to live,

the original plan for an economically self-sufficient community never came to fruition. Production problems prevented the factory from becoming a profitable manufacturing operation, and the building was soon used for other purposes. Many of the city people who came to live in Roosevelt were not inclined to be part-time farmers, and the concept of agricultural self-sufficiency soon disintegrated. The village thrived, however, as a residential community, although its original goals were discarded. Instead of a haven from urban industry, Roosevelt became a refuge for artists and other creative people who appreciated the village's unusual character.

There was very little other construction during the Depression. In 1934 a small impetus was given to the then moribund construction industry by the creation of the Federal Housing Administration (FHA). This body was established to implement the funding of new construction and, thus, to spur the improvement of existing units. Low-interest loans offered by the agency encouraged a modest number of housing starts. The first FHA mortgage was granted for a house in Pompton Plains.

Despite the infusion of FHA money, New Jersey remained essentially depressed until the approach of World War II. As they had for World War I, the state's munitions industries moved into high gear to support a war across the Atlantic. New Jersey's many other areas of manufacturing reopened production lines and, like much of the nation, began to move rapidly toward economic recovery by meeting the needs of the war effort. Economic recovery, however, did not mean new houses. Instead, wartime shortages that included men as well as goods effectively ended all but war-related construction.

The war's end did not bring instant recovery to the construction business. When the lifting of wartime restrictions of goods and materials again permitted the manufacture of consumer goods, demand was so great that there were shortages of everything from toasters to automobiles. Of all the shortages, the most widely publicized and deeply felt was that of housing. It was so severe that people were forced to pay exorbitant rents for the privilege of living in substandard facilities. Families who could afford better often found themselves crowded into very small and often decrepit spaces.

## Mass Production

In order to meet the demand for new, moderately priced housing, builders began to apply mass-production techniques to what had previously been a custom business. The architectural variety and even distinction that characterized earlier developments such as Llewellyn Park and Radburn were sacrificed for economy and efficiency. The result was the major subdivisions that filled many empty spaces near the cities. Rows of simple, often identical, dwellings were built simultaneously on small, also identical, plots of land. Within a few years New Jersey had its own Levittown, the ultimate in mass housing.

The size and character of postwar houses were determined as much by the terms of the available mortgage money as by housing needs and buyer taste. Shortly after the war the G.I. mortgage, available to all those who had served in the armed forces, joined the FHA mortgage as a low-cost source of funds requiring little if any down payment. Because these mortgages were designed for those with limited capital but a dependable income, the terms of the mortgages encouraged the construction of smaller, low-cost homes.

Most such houses cannot be thought of as architecturally significant. Their appearance was often familiar. A good number were Cape Cods and "colonials" whose traditional appearance was brought up to date by the addition of a large plate-glass window in the main room. One of the most common houses was the now ubiquitous split-level. Although it was essentially a new architectural form it did not offer much in the way of style. Instead, its contribution was practical. Buyers liked it because even the smaller versions created a sense of spaciousness by a more open plan and the always-present picture window. Builders liked it because it lacked a structural stairwell or entry hall, and this, combined with the layout, allowed for more space at lower cost. The split-level became a favorite of subdivision builders, and, ultimately, a symbol of middle-class life in postwar America.

The phenomenon of the major subdivision (and its inhabitants) was carefully scrutinized by sociologists, social psychologists, and popular writers. Books, articles, and dissertations recorded the development of what was, essentially, a new way of life. There was concern about the deleterious effects of so many people living in identical or similar houses and interest in how people would react to the need to create an instant community. Sociologist Herbert Gans became one of the first residents of Levittown, New Jersey, in order to gain an insider's view of the development of society in the "new village" and to chart its formation.

The potential problems, however, represent only one possible viewpoint. For many people these houses, like the bungalows and other smaller houses of the twenties, offered the best feasible solution to the need for shelter. Considering the dimension of the demand and the available resources, these were the best that postwar America had to offer. There were other advantages, too. Members of an increasingly mobile society found they could leave their split-level in New Jersey and move into an identical house almost anywhere in America. Their furniture would fit, the children would know where their rooms were, and, as a result of this new architectural conformity, life could continue with only minor interruptions.

## Modern Design

Although most postwar construction reflected rapid and economical solutions to building problems, there were also significant changes in standards and concepts. The new form that ema nated from the Bauhaus, the radical houses designed by Frank Lloyd Wright, and the clean dramatic line of the International Style that first appeared before the war were beginning to influence the character of American architecture. Despite the plethora of undistinguished houses, the work of many American architects reflected a new aesthetic. Although much of this new architecture was seen in industrial and commercial work, house design was also affected.

In 1949 the Museum of Modern Art commissioned Marcel Breuer (b. 1902) to design a house for a typical middle-class American family. The house was then constructed in the Museum Garden, where the public was able to visit the then unusual structure and appreciate the merits of the new design. This was the first experience for many with the spatial harmonies created by a more open interior plan, the use of a large expanse of glass for exterior walls, and the economical, often sparse, balances of the new aesthetic. Mirror-images of this famous house were built in Princeton and Red Bank. Breuer also designed other dwellings in the state, including the faculty residences at the Institute for Advanced Study in Princeton. Here, as in the Museum house, the clean, simple lines and balances that Breuer was known for are effectively displayed, this time in an apartment facility.

Other noted architects also designed homes in New Jersey. In Millstone, a Frank Lloyd Wright house presents a stark masonry façade to the street. Its only embellishment on the side visible to the public is a clerestory window, shielded by pierced wood panels that form a repeated geometric pattern. Its dramatic rear elevation offers stark contrasts with the muted front. Here, the glass walls and horizontal movements for which Wright was famous make a connection between the woods, the Millstone River, and the great open space within. In Glen Ridge, another Wright house creates a deceptively simple appearance from the road but inside includes features such as the built-in furniture that was among Wright's significant contributions to the American house.

Other noteworthy contemporaries have been built in the state. Often they are hidden away on wooded sites where their sweeping glass expanses and dramatic construction interact with their surroundings. Others have been built along the Shore. Here, the treeless open landscape frequently permits travelers uninterrupted views of a variety of interesting contemporary structures interwoven among the more traditional older houses that fill the coastline.

Contemporary New Jersey dwellings, much like those built in the past, sometimes provide insight into lifestyles of the future. In Princeton, Michael Graves, a leading postmodernist, has designed several striking additions to existing homes. Near Hightstown, the instant community of Twin Rivers, a planned-unit development, represents a current way of dealing with the problem of providing shelter for large numbers of people. Here, townhouses and individual dwellings in a mass-produced contemporary mode combine to shelter more than ten thousand residents. Twin Rivers was designed not only to provide housing but also to function as a community complete with schools, shops, banks, industry, and other urban amenities.

Not many miles away, Rossmoor meets another contemporary social residential problem. Here, a pseudo-colonial village was built for people over the age of forty-eight. Although it was not planned to meet the commercial needs of its residents, it does offer recreational and social facilities.

As we approach the twenty-first century our needs in housing continue to change, together with our ability to meet those needs. Although the single-family dwelling, the traditional American "home," is still the American dream, it has become less obtainable. Social and economic changes have made multiple housing more desirable as well as more accessible. The Twin Rivers and the Rossmoors, extrapolations of concepts that began with communities like Llewellyn Park and Radburn, may, in the future, be the best way to provide adequate housing for most of America. Meanwhile, the rich legacy of our houses remains, providing a historical base upon which the future can rest, as well as a connection with our beginnings.

# Towns of Interest

The story that begins with New Jersey's houses continues in its towns. Although many early settlements are only ghostly remnants within the larger cities that have replaced them, dozens of other neighborhoods and, occasionally, entire downtowns appear much as they did long ago.

A few villages and towns are still rich in pre-Revolutionary houses. Even more retain reminders of the late eighteenth and early nineteenth centuries. Most common in New Jersey, and often most interesting, are the dozens of Victorian towns, products of post–Civil War growth and prosperity. New Jersey's Victorian legacy is extensive. It includes not only specimen houses by the thousand, and villages and towns by the dozen, but also churches, factories, parks, and public buildings that reflect other times.

This listing of communities notable for their domestic architecture is a mere sampling. Some towns have been excluded despite their architectural interest because they are very small or remote. Some of New Jersey's oldest and best houses sit alone on country roads, far from anywhere, unmarked by number or road sign. These, too, are not included. In most cases, the wonderful older houses that have been carefully preserved in the larger cities are excluded from this list as well, since they are individual structures that exist, historically isolated, in urban settings.

The profusion of architecturally interesting houses and towns in the state makes it impossible to cite every one, or describe each town in detail. I have not attempted to do that here. Instead, I have tried to provide good starting points, leaving room and time for the personal discoveries that are the special reward for looking at houses in New Jersey. Many significant areas throughout the state have been included in the New Jersey and National Registers of Historic Places. Where applicable these listings have been included for the towns in the following section.

## Allentown

This is one of many New Jersey villages that has experienced little architectural change since the mid-nineteenth century, and the essence of that century pervades it. The town also contains small, vernacular eighteenth-century brick houses and a great many well-preserved frame structures, including an exceptional three-house row that is set between other vintage houses. An excellent late Federal house faces small, relatively uncomplex Victorians.

Roads that lead from the center of town provide interesting architectural contrasts. In one direction there is a concentration of small Victorian vernacular structures. In another direction, Main Street becomes a country road, with buildings more elegant than those in town. Among them, not far from the town center, a pair of outstanding bracketed villas face each other. These prototypical pattern-book houses have the variety of window shapes and bracketed structure that turn cube houses into visually complex forms and make them so attractive. These two are crowned with belvederes pierced by arched windows, elaborated with brackets, and topped by two of the most whimsical finials in New Jersey.

## Alloway

Alloway, a crossroads town in the middle of South Jersey's farmlands, looks as if its last nail had been driven before its men returned from the Civil War. Restrained gingerbread decorates many of the modest houses. A saltbox and other earlier structures contribute to the atmosphere of time past. The open countryside that surrounds Alloway was home to some of the state's earliest residents. Their houses remain, scattered along narrow back roads. Patterned-brick Quaker houses are the most dramatic, but many other eighteenth- and early-nineteenth-century houses stand in the open fields and occasional stands of woodland that are typical of this part of the state.

## Bay Head

Bay Head was established in 1897 by Princetonians in search of fresh summer air. Little of its appearance has changed since its first days. Comfortable seaside "cottages" in the Shingle Style sit close by each other along the beach. Time has darkened their exteriors, intensifying their sense of mass. All the variety that falls within the Shingle nomenclature is apparent here. Dutch and other Colonials and the various versions of Queen Anne with ocean-front balconies and airy porches take advantage of the view and remind us of the pre-air-conditioning era.

The churches and other nonresidential architecture on the single street that is "downtown" Bay Head are also in the Shingle Style, creating unusual architectural homogeneity.

## Belvidere

Exceptional Victorian architecture is interspersed with more modest but interesting vernacular houses of the same period. This pretty Delaware River town, seemingly remote from twentieth-century bustle, conveys the sense of a late-nineteenth-century community. A small park near the commercial area is surrounded by a number of turn-of-the-century dwellings, giving the heart of town a remarkable architectural consistency.

## Blairstown

Blairstown's short main street still has the intimate, slow-paced atmosphere of a nineteenth-century byway. Buildings sit close to the street, and the overhangs of second-story balconies intensify the cozy atmosphere. Small shops, nineteenth-century houses, and a few commercial buildings complete the village. Outlying roads include interesting houses contemporary with those in town. Greek Revivals and a few later vernacular houses are scattered along the roads that wind up the mountains surrounding the town.

## Boonton

A rich vein of iron and a river that could be harnessed for power attracted early settlers to Boonton. On land purchased from the Indians in the beginning of the eighteenth century, ironworks were developed well before the American Revolution. Boonton grew slowly after its initial prosperity. As a result, a diverse architectural legacy has survived. The busy main street, snaking up a hillside, marks the center of a town that is late nineteenth century in all but the nature of its commerce. Surrounding streets reflect over two centuries of house building—former farmhouses, frame Greek Revivals, tiny workers' cottages, a pair of octagons, and several brick Federals. Here and there, a smattering of gingerbread adds to the assortment. A tiny Stick Style church is an architectural high point in the downtown area. The village's periphery and the surrounding township are equally rich in early architecture. A variety of specimen Dutch Colonials include a few that claim late-seventeenth-century origins. German bank houses and early folk and vernacular styles make Boonton and its environs an unusually rich architectural mix.

---

*Boonton Historic District*
19th century
Area includes Main, Church, Brick, Cornelia, and Cedar streets
SR 01/14/80

## Bordentown

When Thomas Farnsworth established his "Landing" at the junction of the Delaware River and the Crosswicks Creek in 1682, he began a settlement that became home to such disparate individuals as Thomas Paine, Benjamin Franklin, Clara Barton, and Joseph Bonaparte, older brother of Napoleon, whose mansion still stands in town.

Joseph Borden acquired most of the town before 1725. By 1740 the enterprising Borden had established a transportation system between New York and

Philadelphia, thus connecting Bordentown with its two most important neighbors. Eighteenth-century prosperity is reflected in the relatively large number of houses that were built before 1800. These houses stand along the entire length of Farnsworth Avenue and are interspersed with excellent early Victorian houses, including simple frame vernaculars and more elaborate brick dwellings.

Continuing nineteenth-century prosperity is apparent in many fine brick and masonry houses. The most famous is a picturesque Italianate structure designed by John Notman, but there is also a profusion of other Italianate houses, Greek Revivals, Federals, and an assortment of modest gingerbread as well as several groups of carefully cared for rowhouses.

Bordentown's prosperity ended when the railroad replaced the Delaware and Raritan Canal as a commercial route. There has been almost no new construction during the past century. The business district evokes the nineteenth century. Although the older municipal buildings are not used for their original purposes, they remain architectural assets. The old city hall, a Victorian glory, testifies to the Victorian penchant for ornament. Carefully preserved classic pilasters, Romanesque arches, and a presumptuous clock tower crowned with a gilded weather vane reflect the glow of an earlier Bordentown.

---

*Bordentown Historic District*
18–19th centuries
Area includes Farnsworth, Second and Third Avenues, Crosswicks, Prince, Walnut, Burlington, Park, and Spring streets
SR 07/07/76

## Burlington

As the capital of West Jersey, Burlington became a city early in its history. As a result, almost all its older structures are urban rowhouses, offering density and character hard to find elsewhere. Much of the center of town is a historic district composed of these early houses. Many have been preserved or restored, and several streets maintain their eighteenth- and early-nineteenth-century appearance. Wood Street, leading to the Delaware River, is bordered by rows of eighteenth-century brick houses interrupted by an occasional frame house, a seventeenth-century dwelling, one of the oldest in New Jersey, and an early-nineteenth-century house that was a haven for the family of Ulysses Grant during the Civil War.

The city also includes eighteenth- and nineteenth-century neighborhoods that have not been restored to their original appearance but offer roof lines, windows, and doorways that reflect their origins.

Good Victorian houses are to be found in Burlington. Entire modest neighborhoods are a delight to consider. High Street boasts a noteworthy Mansard complete with cresting and attractive roof tiling. The Grubb houses, two of the best Second Gothic Revival dwellings in the state, face the Delaware. Their complex polychrome brickwork is complemented by ponderous embellishment. Pointed arches, bargeboards without a hint of whimsey, and a somber front entryway are reminders of the form's churchly origins.

---

*Burlington Historic District*
18–19th centuries
Area includes West Delaware, Wood, and Broad streets
SR 07/01/74 NR 03/13/75

## Califon

Califon's remote location has protected it from twentieth-century intrusion. Although most of the houses are modest, this rural nineteenth-century enclave is remarkable for its period effect. A minute doctor's residence (1881) and pharmacy (1900) remind us of the capacity for whimsey in even the simplest Victorian dwellings.

---

*Califon Historic District*
19–20th centuries
Area includes Main, Academy, Mill, Bank, and First streets, Railroad and Philhower avenues, and River Road
SR 05/08/75 NR 10/14/76

## Cape May City

It is rumored that there were Dutch whalers in Cape May as early as 1630, but no traces of their activity remain. Instead, the state's southernmost city is dominated by a profusion of nineteenth-century structures.

After the war of 1812, steamboat service attracted Southerners to the well-advertised resort, and in 1816 the first grand hotel was built. Cape May remained a major resort until the end of the nineteenth century, when fickle vacationers turned to Long Branch and Atlantic City.

One of the nation's greatest concentrations of Victorian architecture is to be found here. Even an aimless walk around Cape May City will bring you to superb examples of high-style bracketed villas, gingerbread cottages notable for both the quality and quantity of their ornate ornament, Gothic piles with churchlike doors and windows, a specimen Stick Style structure, an octagon, a Queen Anne, and all manner of smaller vernaculars.

Unfortunately, a good deal of the town has fallen victim to its own attractiveness, and as a result of its commercial success many of the best structures have been replaced by less than the best that this century has to offer. Many commercial ventures tarnish the Victorian patina that once graced the entire community.

---

*Cape May Historic District*
circa 1850–1910
Entire city National Historic Landmark
SR 12/10/70 NR 12/29/79

## Cape May Point

This tiny Victorian settlement marks the most southerly point in New Jersey. Settled as a religious community during the nineteenth century, it evolved into a resort area. Great Victorian summer houses once stood along dunes that are no longer there. The powerful rip tides created by the meeting of the Atlantic Ocean and Delaware Bay combined with periodic storms to wash many houses and much of the Point into the ocean. Quite a few nineteenth- and early-twentieth-century houses remain, but these are the more modest dwellings that once sat well back from the shore.

The Point's original religious character is still evident in the form of several Victorian churches and a convent. Each adds architectural interest to the area, but none can match Saint Peter's-by-the-Sea. This fine example of the Stick Style was originally built for the Philadelphia Centennial Exhibition. It was later dismantled and moved to the Point, where it reigns as the supreme architectural ornament.

## Clinton

The South Branch of the Raritan River provided the inland route by which the original settlers reached Clinton. The river also provided the water power that made the area an attractive place to settle. The importance of water power is evidenced by the eighteenth-century mill and its nineteenth-century neighbor in the center of town.

Clinton is remarkable for its variety of architectural style. Even more remarkable are the fine quality and condition of many buildings. The commercial area has made few concessions to the twentieth century; business and recreational activities are conducted in a downtown that has preserved its architectural integrity. The streets that lead to the center of town are equally rich in fine houses that have been respectfully tended. Ornate Victorians, sparkling Greek Revivals, and public buildings that look as they did over a hundred years ago combine with a Victorian center to make this one of the most architecturally interesting communities in the state.

## Cranbury

Cranbury has served as a way station for travelers since 1686. Because of its location between the capitals of the two Jerseys, traffic was heavy enough to support more than one hostelry. The current inn has stood on its site since 1780, but most of the surrounding houses are a few decades younger. Almost every house that lines Main Street was built during the nineteenth century, most before 1850. Like much rural architecture, they are vernacular. Although there are a few more elaborate houses, the outstanding feature of Cranbury is not its individual dwellings but the nineteenth-century atmosphere created by its bright, white houses.

---

*Cranbury Historic District*
18–19th centuries
Area includes Main and Prospect streets, Maplewood and Scott avenues, Bunker Hill Road, Symmes Court, Westminster Place, Park and Wesley places
SR 08/09/79 NR 09/18/80

## Crosswicks

Dozens of small vernacular houses, mainly from the early nineteenth century, surround Crosswicks' large green and meetinghouses. Eighteenth- and nineteenth-century houses sit close by each other on curved, picturesque Main Street, which was once an Indian trail. Almost no intrusion or alteration has marred this tiny settlement. Progress is marked by the occasional bit of gingerbread and by the somewhat grander Tuscan and Second Empire structures on the roads that lead from the center of the village. North Crosswicks, across a narrow bridge and a county line, includes some even older houses and a few good mid-nineteenth-century dwellings, almost isolated in the middle of seemingly endless farmland.

*Crosswicks Historic District*
18–19th centuries
Area includes Chesterfield–Crosswicks Road and Front Street
SR 10/23/75 NR 05/03/76

## Flemington

Although Flemington and its surrounding area were settled in the eighteenth century, it is remarkable for its Victorian architecture. The town centers around a large, ornate hotel with a mansard roof and pillared loggias, an early Greek Revival courthouse, and a Gothic borough hall. Good examples of almost every nineteenth-century style and a few slightly bizarre blends in the best Victorian tradition line Main Street.

Several exceptional houses appear to combine the Victorian desire for ornament with the restraint of Greek Revival. Gilded ornament, grille-covered frieze windows, and elaborate porticoes are made more dramatic by the scale of the supporting columns. Ornate door and window details further enrich these houses. Side streets, too, are essentially nineteenth-century, but with smaller, vernacular versions of the Main Street villas.

*Flemington Historic District*
18–19th centuries
Includes Broad, Main, East Main, North Main, Spring, Court, Bonnell, Mine, William, Brown, Academy, Capner, Church, and Choiristers streets; Park, Bloomfield, Emery, Maple, Grant, Dewey, Hopewell, Pennsylvania, New York, Central, and Lloyd avenues
SR 02/27/80 NR 09/17/80

## Freehold

Freehold's Main Street was once the King's Highway and the old Burlington Trail, and Freehold's architecture reflects its history. There are interesting early houses throughout the area, but the town is mainly of the late nineteenth century. Despite bustling commerce and a large commercial center, it has kept the ambiance of that period, even along the busiest streets. A variety of roof lines, towers, ornate trim, elaborate porches and doorways, balconies, brackets, and gingerbread adorn dozens of nineteenth-century houses. A pair of Classic Revival houses in the temple form can be seen in the busiest section of Main Street. An Italianate villa, a near duplicate of a design from Downing's *Cottage Residences*, can be found on Broad Street. Bracketed villas with Greek Revival details and a good example of Richardsonian Shingle complete the architectural parade.

## Greenwich

New Jersey's own tea party took place in Greenwich in 1774. Many of the houses that were standing on the night of the tea burning are still to be seen along Great Street. The wide avenue, planned by John Fenwick as "Ye Greate Street," was originally designed for sixteen-acre estates. Although many of the houses are located on smaller plots, the tiny village has a spacious, rustic feeling.

Nearly all the early houses that were built in Greenwich still stand. Manor houses, a stone tavern, some tiny frame structures, and several brick ones, all in fine repair, offer examples of the subtle variety to be found in pre-Revolutionary vernacular houses. There are also simple versions of later styles. The residents are proud of the quality of their architecture, and the result is unusual in both the total effect of the community and the fine condition of the many historic dwellings. Greenwich is not so much a village as an island of houses set deep in the open areas of southwestern New Jersey. Like most early towns, it borders a river; unlike most of the state's early communities, it has remained rural.

---

*Greenwich Historic District*
17–19th centuries
Main Street, from the Cohansey River north to Othello
SR 11/30/71 NR 01/20/72

## Hackettstown

Although Hackettstown can trace its history to the early eighteenth century, its wealth of fine nineteenth-century houses is exceptional. Main Street, a long, busy thoroughfare, includes well-preserved hotels, churches, and community buildings from the first half of that century. Surrounding streets are filled with later Victorian dwellings, most carefully maintained or restored. An enormous variety of style and ornament can be seen in nineteenth-century neighborhoods extending several blocks. A brick octagon house, elegant mansard roofs, and the rich combinations of color tones characteristic of Victorian dwellings are reminders of a nineteenth-century world.

## Haddonfield

In Haddonfield you can stand on the King's Highway and see the same houses that were standing when the Continental Congress met here in 1777. Situated close to Philadelphia, Haddonfield was an important way station between Salem and Burlington. In the center of town, pre-Revolutionary architecture survives in fine condition. The oldest house, a tiny gambrel-roofed cottage, is thought to date from 1710; its neighbors are nearly as old. Fine brick Federal houses, too, can be seen in the oldest part of town, together with an early meetinghouse.

---

*Haddonfield Historic District*
18–20th centuries
Area includes sections of King's Highway; Tanner, Lake, Grove, Chestnut, Centre, Potter, Clement, and Mechanic streets; Warwick Road, Washington, Colonial, Friends, Lincoln, West Park, East Park, East Atlantic, and West Cottage avenues
SR 04/18/80

## Hightstown

When Samuel Sloan (1815–1884) built his exceptional bracketed villa on Main Street, he chose Hightstown for its convenient location, midway between Perth Amboy and Burlington. Many other people apparently felt the same way, for the area across from the Peddie School boasts a great number of fine houses built after 1850. The octagon is outstanding, and other good vernacular Victorians fill the neighborhood. Stockton Street is also lined with fine homes from the period. A variety of ornament is found not only on the Victorians but in many cases as later additions on the surviving eighteenth-century houses.

## Hoboken

Time has been much more generous with Hoboken than with surrounding urban communities. This carefully cared for square mile, located on a bluff overlooking the Hudson River and New York City, has changed very little since its rows of brownstone and brick houses were first built. It is possible to look down Washington Street, the main commercial avenue, and contemplate an unbroken line of façades virtually unaltered since the beginning of this century. Although they appear identical at first glance, their individuality is expressed in the window surrounds, doorways, and cornices that mirror the range of styles in "country houses" of the period. Romanesque, Italianate, Second Empire, and Renaissance Revival trim break the long rows of windows and doors that are often framed with complex sculptural design.

The urban mansions near Stevens Institute offer more complex and elaborate versions of Victorian style than their middle-class neighbors. Mansard roofs, cresting, and seemingly endless ornament are rendered in monumental materials that reflect the weighty importance of the "gentlemen" who built these houses almost one hundred years ago.

## Hope

Moravians came from Pennsylvania in 1774 to establish this tiny village. Although they departed soon after, they left behind a group of buildings, now designated a historic district, that reflected their communal way of life. A *Gemeinhaus* (community house), the Single Sisters Choir (a residence for unmarried women), a large grist mill, and a number of individual dwellings were all built of stone. German vernacular forms are apparent in roughly cut stone, finer cut blocks for quoins, and tall roofs on the smaller dwellings. Although later dwellings have filled in some of the spaces, the center of Hope around High and Union Streets has preserved a moment in architectural time.

## Hopewell

The Hopewell Railroad station, a Second Empire delight, has kept Sunday painters and calendar designers busy for decades. It is the architectural focus of a village of vernacular houses that were built about the same time as the station. Modest amounts of gingerbread, mansard roofs, diffident Gothics, and other restrained Victoriana harmonize with storefronts and church façades. The most conspicuous—and possibly the most interesting—house in this quiet village was purple at the time of this writing. Located on a side street, this cube Italian structure has simple lines embellished by serpentine cartouches topping its windows; its steamboat Gothic spindles and curves are painted white like icing on an enormous birthday cake.

## Island Heights

Tiny pattern-book houses and a few larger dwellings form a miniature Victorian resort on a wooded hillside above the Toms River. It was developed in the late nineteenth century by the Methodist Camp Meeting Association. Although there are now quite a few more recent houses, much of Island Heights illustrates the spectrum of Victorian style on a small scale. Petite Queen Annes, tiny Carpenter Gothics, examples of Stick Style, and insouciant blends are frequently garnished with elaborate porches topped by proportionately minute witches' caps, cupolas, and turrets. Board-and-batten candy stripes, elaborate bargeboards, and ornate brackets embellish well-kept houses that often bear the date of their construction.

Larger Queen Annes and Shingles stand closer to the water. Here verandas and balconies, towers, and patterns created by complex combinations of shingle work adorn structures that are often encircled by porches providing views of the river, Barnegat Bay, and the barrier beach beyond.

## Jersey City

Little has happened in this century to alter the architectural character of the miles of rowhouses that make up a large part of Jersey City. Although the passage of time is evident in some of the neighborhoods, most of the houses, sometimes entire squares or districts, have kept their original appearance.

Most of these houses are superficially similar. Row upon row of brownstone and brick houses distinguish themselves from their neighbors by the variety of ornament that surrounds doorways and windows, adorns cornices, and decorates stairways and walls. Acanthus leaves, heads of gods and goddesses, and grillework that would delight the most demanding Victorian provide architectural delights.

On Jersey Avenue, an unusual row of houses is fronted with delicate cast ironwork of steps and porches that lends an antebellum air to the urban scene. Not far away, Hamilton Park, a quiet square, is almost completely surrounded by brick city houses, creating an urban portrait of another era.

Many of the houses on Bergen Hill, an attractively designed Victorian neighborhood, retain their original grandeur. A row of houses near the top of the hill offers a different cityscape from its neighbors. Here are grander rowhouses with Romanesque arches, bays, balconies, and elaborate dormers. Although the surrounding neighborhood shows a good deal of wear and tear, these once elegant houses form the center of a district that offers a relatively undisturbed image of the past.

---

*Van Vorst Historic District*
19–20th centuries
Area includes Jersey Avenue, Varick, Barrow, Grove, Wayne, Mercer, Montgomery, York, Bright, and Grand streets
SR 08/02/78 NR 03/05/80

*Hamilton Park Historic District*
19th century
Area includes 6th, 7th, 8th, and 9th streets at Hamilton Park
SR 04/27/78 NR 01/25/79

*Paulus Hook Historic District*
19th century
Area includes portions of York, Grand, Sussex, Morris, Essex, Greene, Washington, Warren, and Van Vorst streets/avenues
SR 08/07/81

## Lambertville

In the eighteenth century a ferryboat crossed the Delaware at Lambertville. Washington also crossed the Delaware near here on his way to rout the British at Trenton in 1776. But Lambertville is primarily a Victorian town. The great majority of its houses and commercial structures were built soon after the middle of the nineteenth century. Despite much commercial activity, Main Street today retains its nineteenth-century character. Storefronts and public buildings, including an inn with rocker-bedecked front porch, reflect other days. The houses, which frequently are smaller versions of high-style villas, reflect Victorian desire for ornament and stylistic variety. Dozens of modest dwellings are adorned with turrets, mansard roofs, Tuscan ornament, and an assortment of gingerbread porches. Almost no twentieth-century intrusions interrupt the residential neighborhoods that occupy several blocks near the river.

## Lawrenceville

Before the Revolution, Lawrenceville, then called Maidenhead, was a small village on the stage route between New York and Trenton. Main Street, which is relatively free of commerce, is lined with manor houses as well as smaller frame dwellings that have changed little from the days when Cornwallis and his soldiers passed on their way to Trenton and the famous battle.

There are several good stone Georgian and Federal houses. The most spectacular is the Theophilous Phillips house, a stone mansion built well before the Revolutionary War. Other fine houses can also be seen along the many roads leading to the village. Nearly all these roads were in existence over two hundred years ago, and the many dozens of houses that were then standing have survived. Many of them, with Greek Revival and Victorian wings, document the passage of time, but they have kept enough of their original form to be easily recognized as survivors from an even earlier period.

---

*Lawrence Township Historic District*
18–19th centuries
Lawrenceville; area includes both sides of U.S. Route 206
SR 07/31/72 NR 09/14/72

## Long Branch

Long Branch was once the most splendid seaside resort in America. Today, monolithic condominiums and small, often gaudy commercial establishments have replaced most of the great houses and hotels. At one time the entire shore was lined with enormous beachfront "cottages." Now only two remain, sandwiched between parking lots and high-rise dwellings on the main road through town. Stables and carriage houses that once served the big houses still remain, converted to summer residences. Much of their original appearance has been obscured by asbestos siding and other concessions to time, climate, and changing taste.

Farther inland, a good deal of the earlier architectural grandeur survives. Monmouth College includes two important mansions within its boundaries. One is the former Guggenheim estate, a Louis XVI re-creation designed by Carrère and Hastings. Now a library, much of its original elegance remains. Shadow Lawn, once Woodrow Wilson's summer White House, was rebuilt after a fire in the late twenties. Although it is no longer the same house from which Wilson ran the nation, it is still a good example of the splendor once found in American dwellings. Many good but more modest turn-of-the-century houses also remain, including some by major architects.

## Maplewood and the Oranges

The foothills of the Watchung Mountains were irresistible to those seeking attractive sites for picturesque homes during the nineteenth and early twentieth centuries. West Orange's Llewellyn Park, Davis's garden suburb, is a glamorous and significant grouping of houses but is, unfortunately, not open to the public. In Maplewood and South Orange, the steeply sloping streets between Ridgewood and Wyoming avenues are more accessible and are filled with fine houses mostly built between 1890 and 1930. Half-timbered "Tudor" mansions, dignified Colonials, Shingles, and an occasional chateau mix with eccentric architectural fancies. The area above Wyoming Avenue also includes an occasional dramatic contemporary, most notably a secluded house in Maplewood designed by Frank Lloyd Wright's studio.

## Matawan

During the nineteenth century, seacaptains chose Matawan as a place to live because of its nearness to the Atlantic. On Main Street they built grand houses with turrets and towers. Many such houses still stand, often near dwellings built in the eighteenth century. These earlier houses, including some that predate the Revolution, fill the town with a good array of detail, including the fine curved shingle of the Burrowes mansion, a 1723 dwelling, and the elaborate trim that embellishes the Italianate mansions. Although Matawan is small, examples of Greek Revival, Federal, and the other early styles can also be seen.

## Mauricetown

Victorian prosperity combined with the New England influence to shape this isolated South Jersey riverside village. Although the town was settled in the early 1700s, it was in the nineteenth century that three brothers came from New England, bringing their own builder, and developed a good part of the tiny town. The location encouraged the growth of shipyards that built oyster boats and coastal schooners. The Atlantic shipping created the affluence that allowed seacaptains and prosperous businessmen to build handsome frame houses here. The nineteenth-century village remains, well cared for, with brightly painted houses embellished with elaborate ironwork porches, mansard roofs, complex brackets, bay windows, and Gothic elements.

## Medford

Much of the area that is now Medford Township was a collection of crossroad villages and country farms before the Revolution. The town itself has only a few very early buildings. Most of the houses and the commercial structures were built during the nineteenth century. Many of the older buildings have become municipal offices or businesses, but their exteriors remain as they were, and the center of the town has an air of the early nineteenth century, as do the side streets. Although some of the houses have been enlarged or altered, enough of the original character remains throughout this modest village to create a fine picture of country life as it once was.

## Mendham

Mendham experienced much of its growth before 1800. Its tiny commercial area along Route 24 centers around the Black Horse Inn, which has been in continuous operation since 1742. Phoenix house, once an eighteenth-century hotel, now contains municipal offices. The village that was eighteenth-century Mendham remains today, albeit with a glaze of twentieth-century commerce. Many of the older dwellings have been converted into shops but retain much of their original character despite the merchandise in the windows.

## Middletown

An English land claim dated 1664 makes Middletown one of the oldest New Jersey settlements under English jurisdiction, and it bears the further distinction of being the first permanent English settlement in the colony. There are a few late-seventeenth-century houses and many later but still pre-Revolutionary structures scattered through the Navesink Hills, which surround the center of the city. Along densely wooded roads are clusters of houses that were early villages. Many eighteenth-century dwellings are identified by road markers; others wait to be discovered. The greatest concentration of historic houses can be found on King's Highway, a wide avenue planned in 1719. Many of these houses are small and simple, in the early English or Dutch traditions.

*King's Highway District*
18–19th centuries
King's Highway intersection with State Route 35
SR 12/20/73 NR 05/03/74

*Navesink Historic District*
18–19th centuries
Area including Navesink, Monmouth, and Hillside avenues
SR 10/21/74 NR 09/05/75

## Montclair

The streets of Montclair form one of the largest and best collections of turn-of-the-century architectural elegance that New Jersey has to offer. Easy commuting to Wall Street, along with the late-Victorian desire for grandiose places of residence, produced acres and acres of mansions, mini-estates, larger-than-life "cottages," and a profusion of enormous half-timbered "stockbroker Tudors." On the mountain north and west of the center of town, splendid houses sit at the end of curving drives, surrounded by sweeping, carefully landscaped lawns. Montclair was settled two centuries before these houses were built, and a few of the earliest buildings, such as the Israel Crane house, remain, but it is the balconies, turrets, witches' caps, Palladian ornament, and carefully painted multicolor Second Empire houses that make Montclair special.

## Morristown

The modern structures at the Green in the center of Morristown surround one of the few surviving commons in the state. Morristown Green was marked out by English settlers in 1715. Since that time many significant events have taken place in the area, and many structures remain to document these activities. Evidence of Revolutionary activities includes the huts at Jockey Hollow, the simple Tempe Wick house, the Ford mansion that housed General Washington, and dozens of other dwellings that sheltered officers and men during the winters of 1776–77 and 1779–80. In nearby Morris Plains stands Craftsman Farms, where Gustav Stickley lived and supervised *The Craftsman,* the magazine that did much to reshape American architecture in the early years of this century.

During the second half of the nineteenth century, Morristown became a place for rich people to live. Just before the turn of the century the millionaire population was close to one hundred. In the countryside of Morris Township the millionaires and their almost-as-rich neighbors built splendid dwellings, large enough and expensive enough to affirm their place in the world. An excellent if somewhat more modest Victorian enclave exists south of Green. A registered historic district, this section includes several blocks of good late-nineteenth-century vernacular houses and a few more splendid structures.

---

*Morristown Historic District*
19–20th centuries
Area includes Green, South, DeHart, Elm, Wetmore, Madison, and Pine streets, MacCulloch, Maple, and Colles avenues, Farragut Place, and South Park Place
SR 09/06/73 NR 10/30/73

## Mount Holly

Red brick is the primary construction material in this South Jersey town. Superbly maintained brick buildings border Mount Holly's High Street. The eighteenth-century courthouse and the Friends' meetinghouse are surrounded by dwellings built at the same time and a few years later. The section around High Street, the oldest part of town and a designated historic district, offers an almost uninterrupted journey into the architectural past. Brick sidewalks complete the picture created by fine pre-Revolutionary houses and elegant Georgians and Federals.

Excellent examples of houses from other periods can also be found in Mount Holly. One of the few remaining Swedish board-and-mortar cabins has been moved and restored and is now located near the local hospital. The Ashurst mansion, near the edge of town, is an exceptional example of a Victorian Gothic villa, a near duplicate of "An American Country House of the first class," designed by Gervase Wheeler, in Downing's *Architecture of Country Houses*. At the other end of the spectrum are good examples of workers' houses, some well-preserved Carpenter Gothics, and many fine vernacular versions of most of the significant nineteenth-century styles.

---

*Mount Holly Historic District*
18–19th centuries
Area includes Mill, Pine, High, Garden, White, Union, Bispham, Madison, Buttonwood, Branch, Church, and Ridgeway streets, Park Drive, and Commerce Place
SR 08/07/22 NR 02/20/73

## Newark

The variety of style that lends excitement to urban architecture is apparent in Newark, whose location next to the harbor and proximity to New York City made it an important city from its first days as a Puritan settlement. As a leading industrial city in the nineteenth century Newark continued to grow and prosper. It became home to affluent manufacturers as well as to thousands of laborers. Ferries, and, much later, a tunnel made Newark an attractive residence for those who worked across the Hudson River. As a result, nineteenth-century townhouses, mansions, and thousands of rowhouses line Newark's streets.

Although the city has experienced a great deal of decay during recent decades, good examples of nineteenth-century domestic urban style remain. Entire neighborhoods of brownstones, brick rowhouses, and large turn-of-the century single-family residences illustrate the variety of design and ornament characteristic of the era. Many of these neighborhoods are, in fact, architectural ghosts, in that they are no longer cared for and some of the houses have reached an advanced state of decay. But even these houses provide a good picture of Victorian taste through their carved and cast ornament, hood moldings, doorways, and stained glass.

Forest Hill retains its affluent suburban character. Here, late nineteenth-century villas are surrounded by carefully tended lawns and tall trees. Lincoln Park, once a colonial pasture and later, a grand city neighborhood, has not fared as well, but a few excellent houses still surround this mid-city triangle of green and provide a picture of the good life during the last century. James Street Commons, near the Newark Museum, includes dozens of homes in various stages of both decay and rehabilitation. Bricks, brownstones, and some older frame structures span over a century of urban living.

---

*James Street Commons Historic District*
19–20th centuries
Area includes High, University, Bleeker, New, Linden, James, Essex, Burnet, Washington, and Summit streets, Central Avenue
SR 02/10/77 NR 01/09/78

## New Brunswick

Contemporary New Brunswick contains almost no evidence of the Dutch and English settlers who arrived there at the end of the seventeenth century. The most tangible reminder of the past is Albany Street, which was given its name by Dutch who migrated here from Albany, New York. There is also very little of the eighteenth century to be seen, although the city was the scene of much activity at that time. Nineteenth-century architecture has fared better. A few Federal houses and some excellent Greek Revivals represent the first half of the century, but it is the later houses that set New Brunswick's style. The town is dominated by hundreds of modest three-bay houses with restrained ornament, but there are several more elegant neighborhoods. The Italianate Bishop house in the center of Rutgers University is exceptional: round-arched windows, a square tower, and an asymmetrical silhouette combine to create an elegant high-style house. Neighboring houses surrounding the campus are nearly as fine. Although many have been absorbed by the university and fraternities, they still retain much of their original grandeur. Livingston Avenue and its surrounding streets offer a good view of a late Victorian neighborhood.

---

*Hiram Market Historic District*
19th century
Albany, Bayard, Church, Dennis, Hiram, Memorial Parkway, Nielson, Paterson, Peace, and Richmond streets
SR 06/25/80

## Newton

In Newton's town square stands a monument "erected by a grateful people to the services and sacrifices of soldiers and sailors in the war of rebellion." The square is surrounded by a heroically scaled Greek Revival courthouse and a row of nineteenth-century commercial structures so richly embellished and neatly arranged that it is difficult to remember that this is the late twentieth century. Nearby, on Main Street, is an array of fine Victorian structures, including one of the most interesting late-nineteenth-century houses in the state. The Merriam house, now a home for the aged, boasts an unusual variety of ornament, balconies, gables, cupolas, and the countless variations on a single structural theme that late Victorian architects did so well. Other houses throughout Newton seem to have drawn inspiration from their grand neighbor, and porches, spindlework, roof lines, ornate shingling, and other Victorian expressions of form highlight the side streets.

## Ocean Grove

The entire village of Ocean Grove has changed little since the days when it was planned as a Methodist summer retreat in 1869. Rows of tents still serve as summer quarters, and the enormous auditorium where Caruso once sang is still used for public functions. Although the tent community alone would make Ocean Grove noteworthy as a residential community, an abundance of gingerbread and other good Victorian ornament also distinguish this town.

Almost all the houses in Ocean Grove were built during the first decade of its existence. These include tiny cottages that were probably pattern-book-inspired, and simple, medium-sized houses made eloquent by an endless array of porches, balconies, and complex ornament. Modern weatherproof materials mask some of the original surfaces, and gingerbread has been stripped from a few of the houses to cope with seaside weather, but even these simplified structures are marked by the complex silhouettes of their era. Although one is aware of gaps, the concentration of good Victorian houses surrounded by public and commercial areas, also of the last century, makes Ocean Grove one of the finer examples of Victoriana in New Jersey.

## Pennington

Before there were colonists, Indians traveled the roads that pass through Pennington. Years later, travelers between Trenton and Flemington also passed through here. The houses in this small community reflect its long history. Pre-Revolutionary structures, Federals, Greek Revivals, and vernacular Victorians are close by each other, frequently in proper chronologic sequence, fanning out from the crossroads at the center of town. Because Pennington has always been a farm community, many of the early houses are on roads that lead through the surrounding countryside.

The railroad came through Pennington in the 1830s, but it did not bring the rapid growth that took place elsewhere. Large, prosperous farms protected the area, and, although there is at least one example of most nineteenth-century styles, the Victorian architectural population is modest. Outstanding are two imposing Shingle Queen Annes. Turrets, porches, and other structural complexities combine to make both buildings interesting.

## Plainfield

Plainfield dates back to colonial days, but its present character was determined when the railroad came through. In the first half of the nineteenth century, trains made it possible for bankers and brokers to build grand houses from which they could commute, and examples of the architectural richness that reflected their lives still fill many of Plainfield' s streets. Few additions or alterations interrupt the period grandeur; dazzling combinations of shingle work, stone, brick, and frame remain. Although some of the houses have given way to garden apartments and other "modern improvements," hundreds of eyebrow windows, witches' caps, Romanesque arches, terra cotta ornaments, Oriental flower motifs, Eastlake turnings, and blends that appear to have come directly from some misguided owner's ego create an extraordinary architectural display.

---

*Crescent Area Historic District*
19th century
Crescent Avenue; 1st, 2nd, and 3rd place; Park Avenue between Crescent Avenue and 9th Street; 9th Street between Park Avenue and Watchung

Avenue; Watchung Avenue between 7th and 9th Streets; 7th Street between Watchung Avenue, 9th Street, and Franklin Place
SR 08/15/80 NR 12/12/80

## Princeton

The trees are taller and the farmland has filled in with woods, homes and campuses, but the houses that General Washington and his men passed still stand close by the roadside. Many are either preserved or restored to their original appearance.

There are also outstanding examples of later style. Excellent Georgians and Federals built of brick, stone, frame, and stucco remain from post-Revolutionary days. Greek Revival architecture, too, is notable in Princeton. Both sides of Alexander Road are lined with Greek Revivals designed and built by Charles Steadman. These are remarkable for their classic austerity tempered by fine ornament. The concentration of one style within a single area is an unusual phenomenon.

There is little Victorian style, but turn-of-the-century grandeur can be seen in the town's western section, where elegant houses of the various revivals occupy block after block. Renaissance palazzos, Dutch cottages, Gothic Revivals, and an embarrassment of "colonial" riches fill this neighborhood. Princeton also has a sampling of good contemporaries, often tucked into the wooded hillsides that edge the town.

---

*Princeton Historic District*
18–20th centuries
Area encompasses Mercer, Nassau, Prospect, Williams, Stockton, Wiggins, and Olden streets, Alexander, Springdale, and College roads, Lovers Lane, and Library Place
SR 10/29/73 NR 06/28/75

## Radburn

Radburn was one of America's first planned garden suburbs. It was designed to be self-contained, large enough to support necessary services yet small enough to form a satisfactory social unit for its residents. Radburn is distinguished by the manner in which its residential units have been grouped around a central, landscaped open space sited to make the automobile as unobtrusive as possible. Although houses are closely grouped on cul-de-sacs that admit cars, their rear façades open on to large common areas rather than traditional back yards. The houses, in a variety of stylistic adaptations, were designed with attractive prospects facing the common areas.

Although postwar Fairlawn now surrounds Radburn, the original qualities of the community still exist. Landscaped common areas are marked with winding walks, tunnels obviate the need for crossing streets, and the clustered residences emanate a sense of coziness and community.

---

*Radburn Historic District*
1929
Area includes Fair Lawn, Berdan, and Prospect avenues, Plaza and Radburn roads
SR 10/15/74 NR 04/16/75

## Rancocas

All of the houses in this unusual, remote village are built of brick. The meetinghouse and a few other structures date back to colonial days, when Rancocas was a Quaker settlement. Most of the simple red bricks, however, were built in the late eighteenth and early nineteenth centuries. The date of construction of each house can be seen on the front wall. These houses include modest versions of Federal, Colonial, Greek Revival, and Gothic styles.

---

*Rancocas Historic Village*
18–19th centuries
Area includes Main, Bridge, Wills, and Second streets
SR 09/06/73 NR 06/05/75

## Riverton

In 1851 a group of sailing enthusiasts from Philadelphia crossed the Delaware and built elegant river-front manor houses. Many of these grand structures were designed by Samuel Sloan, a noted architect of the time. The surrounding community, which formed soon after, contains vernacular examples of most major Victorian styles. Although nineteenth-century houses shape the town's character, several earlier structures from its rural eighteenth-century days still stand among their more elaborate neighbors.

## Roosevelt

Bauhaus-inspired cinderblock houses were built during the 1930s to create the town originally known as Jersey Homesteads, which was designed as a social experiment in cooperative living for needle-trade workers. The village included a factory as well as several dozen flat-roofed houses in the functional, unadorned manner typical of the Bauhaus style. Although the factory soon failed and the village never became economically self-sufficient, it attracted artists and writers who enjoyed the architectural ambience of this unusual experiment. Today the village retains almost all its original character despite the addition of the occasional second story or wing to some houses.

## Rumson

Unlike many New Jersey shore communities, Rumson has preserved almost all its early elegance. The barrier beach at Sea Bright and an absence of commerce have stood in the way of "progress." Many of the manor houses that were built in the late nineteenth and early twentieth centuries still stand, albeit on reduced acreage and often without the stables, tennis courts, and outbuildings that once made the estates into minor fiefdoms.

Carrère and Hastings, Stanford White, and the firm of McKim, Mead and White were among the important American architects who designed Rumson's houses. Although many houses have been altered or "modernized," they still convey a sense of grandeur. Quiet, well-landscaped streets are bordered by fine newer homes that were built when the estates sold off parcels of land, but winding drives still lead through small landscaped parks to houses that reflect another way of life.

## Salem

The brick pavements of Salem's Market Street Historic District lead through an architectural panorama that spans more than a century of American dwelling styles. The oldest houses date from pre-Revolutionary times and include a proper "South Jersey brick" with Flemish bond brickwork that was built during the first quarter of the eighteenth century. Although almost all the houses have been somewhat modified over the centuries, dozens that are crowded into the two-block historic district maintain much of their original appearance. Federals, Greek Revivals, Gothics, a saltbox, and a variety of Victorians reflect the town's early affluence.

Although the houses on West Broadway have not yet been named a historic district, they, too, are elegant examples of their genre. They are mainly larger and grander than their Market Street contemporaries and reflect the prosperity of Salem, once one of the major ports of entry in the colonies.

---

*Market Street Historic District*
18–19th centuries
Area includes 9–119 Market Street, and East Broadway
SR 12/09/74 NR 04/10/75

## Shrewsbury

The crossroads that was once most of Shrewsbury is located at the intersection of two King's Highways, each originally part of an Indian trail. Although the crossroads is now known as the intersection of Broad Street and Sycamore Avenue, much of the early atmosphere remains. Standing close to the intersection are a frame 1816 Friends' meetinghouse, an old burying ground, Old Christ Church that still bears Revolutionary bullet holes and an iron British crown on its spire, and the late Greek Revival Presbyterian Church. The Allen house, also at the crossroads, dates from about 1750 and was a tavern before the Revolution. During the war it was the scene of much activity. The house, outbuildings, and gardens have been restored, providing an attractive focus for the remains of one of the first English settlements in the colony.

## Spring Lake

Towers, turrets, finials, and other pointed ornaments reach skyward from grand hotels and splendid seaside "cottages" and villas. Substantial turn-of-the-century houses are surrounded by porches with their own minor towers.

In the center of town are a business district and a park enclosing a small lake. The Victorian atmosphere continues with rustic fencing and a matching bridge that reflect the love of the "natural" that characterized the Victorian ideal.

## Trenton

Were it not for pressure from the southern states-to-be, the seat of American government would still be in Trenton. In 1784, the Continental Congress, meeting at Trenton, chose that city to be the nation's capital. Although this never came to be, Trenton did become the capital of New Jersey and a leading manufacturing city.

Barracks built during the French and Indian War remain in the very heart of the city, near the capitol building designed by John Notman. General Washington and his officers were entertained in several still-standing early houses. Other surviving eighteenth- and early-nineteenth-century structures include dwellings, factories, and public buildings.

The State House Historic District and surrounding streets include late-eighteenth- and early-nineteenth-century dwellings and some fine late-Victorian town houses. A ponderous masonry Richardsonian Romanesque reigns not far from Federal frame vernaculars.

One of the most interesting older residential concentrations is the Mill Hill Mercer-Jackson area near the center of the city. A well-kept nineteenth-century neighborhood that has been restored, it includes an array of urban styles, brick sidewalks, and gaslit streets.

---

*Berkeley Square Historic District*
circa 1890–1910
Parkside, Riverside, and Overbrook avenues, and West State Street (both sides)
SR 03/12/80 NR 11/10/80

*Chambersburg Historic District*
Area includes South Clinton, Mott, Hudson, Swan, Emory, Fulton, and Dye streets
SHPO Opinion: 01/08/81

*Mill Hill Historic District*
Area includes East Front, Mercer, Jackson, Market, Livingston, Clay, and Broads streets, and Greenwood Avenue
SR 04/13/77 NR 12/12/77

# Glossary

*architrave:* Lowest element of entablature.
*bargeboard:* Trim along lower edge of gable roof; originally carved board; later scroll-sawn flat designs.
*bay:* Building unit defined by repeated columns, pilasters, or other framing elements.
*belvedere:* Tower or turret built primarily to provide viewing point.
*board-and-batten:* Typically Gothic Revival sheathing for frame buildings: wide boards (usually vertical) whose joints are covered by narrower strips called battens.
*bracket:* Projecting device placed under cornices, balconies, windows, or eaves; can be functional or purely decorative.
*cornice:* Uppermost part of entablature.
*cresting:* Ornamental ridging on roof.
*cupola:* Small domelike structure on roof or tower.
*dentil:* Small rectangular block used in series to form molding below a cornice.
*entablature:* Horizontal part of classical order, above columns or pilasters.
*fanlight:* Elliptical or semicircular window over a door.
*finial:* Ornament at peak of tower, gable, or spire.
*frieze:* Middle part of entablature, between architrave and cornice.
*gambrel roof:* Roof with two slopes of different pitch flanking ridge.
*grille:* Metal grating forming screen, usually decorative; also window with such grating.
*half timbering:* Frame construction in which wood is exposed and space between wood filled with brick or stucco. In American architecture, decorative rather than functional.
*header:* Brick or stone laid with end toward face of wall.
*hood molding:* Large projecting molding over window.
*lintel:* Load-bearing beam or support between columns or walls.
*pediment:* Gable end of Classical temple; more generally, any cornice-framed door or window crown.
*pilaster:* Flat-faced representation of column.
*port cochère:* Covered area attached to house; used to provide shelter for those leaving or arriving in carriages.
*portico:* Porch, with roof usually supported by columns.
*quoin:* Structural or decorative masonry or wood block at corner of building.
*stretcher:* Brick or stone laid with length parallel to face of wall.
*turret:* Small tower.
*vergeboard:* Bargeboard.

# Suggested Readings


## General

Andrews, Wayne. *Architecture, Ambition, and Americans*. New York, 1964.

Eberlein, Harold, and Hubbard, Cortland. *American Georgian Architecture*. Bloomington, Ind., 1952.

Fitch, James Marston. *American Building: The Historical Forces That Shaped It*. 2nd ed. Boston, 1966.

Gowans, Alan. *Images of American Living: Four Centuries of Architecture and Furniture as Cultural Expression*. Philadelphia, 1964.

Hamlin, Talbot. *Greek Revival Architecture in America*. New York, 1944.

Kidder-Smith, G. E. *A Pictorial History of Architecture in America*. 2 vols. New York, 1976.

Kidney, Walter C. *The Architecture of Choice: Eclecticism in America*. Boston, 1975.

Kimball, S. Fiske. *Domestic Architecture of the American Colonies and of the Early Republic*. New York, 1922.

Loth, Calder, and Sadler, Julius T., Jr. *The Only Proper Style: Gothic Architecture in America*. Boston, 1975.

Maass, John. *The Gingerbread Age: A View of Victorian America*. New York, 1957.

Rifkind, Carol. *A Field Guide to American Architecture*. New York, 1980.

Roth, Leland M. *A Concise History of American Architecture*. New York, 1979.

Scully, Vincent. *The Shingle Style: Architectural Theory and Design from Richardson to the Origins of Wright*. New Haven, 1955.

Whiffen, Marcus. *American Architecture Since 1780: A Guide to the Styles*. Cambridge, Mass, 1969.

Whiffen, Marcus, and Koeper, Frederic. *American Architecture 1607–1976*. Cambridge, Mass., 1981.

## New Jersey

Bailey, Rosalie, F. *Pre-Revolutionary Dutch Houses and Families in Northern New Jersey and Southern New York*. New York, 1936.

Greiff, Constance, Gibbons, Mary W., and Menzies, Elizabeth G. C. *Princeton Architecture*. Princeton, 1967.

Newberry, Lida, ed. *New Jersey: A Guide to Its Present and Past*. New York, 1977.

Rifkind, Carol, and Levine, Carol. *Mansions, Mills, and Main Streets: Buildings and Places to Explore Within 50 Miles of New York City*. New York, 1975.

Thomas, George E., and Doebley, Carl. *Cape May: Queen of the Seaside Resorts*. Cranbury, N.J., 1976.


For more specific listings of individual houses and districts see the national and New Jersey registers of historic places. Books and guides to local architecture and history are frequently available from county cultural and heritage commissions, local historical societies, and libraries.